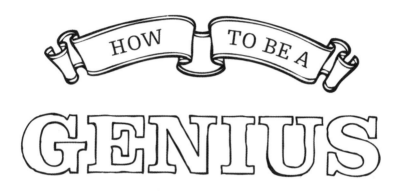

HOW TO BE A GENIUS

First published in the United Kingdom in 2011 by
Collins & Brown
10 Southcombe Street
London
W14 0RA

An imprint of Anova Books Company Ltd

Distributed in the United States and Canada by
Sterling Publishing Co, 387 Park Avenue South, New York, NY 10016-8810, USA

ISBN 978-184340-638-9

A CIP catalogue record for this book is available from the British Library.

10 9 8 7 6 5 4 3 2 1

Printed and bound by 1010 Printing International Ltd. China

This book can be ordered direct from the publisher at www.anovabooks.com

1010 Printing International Limited

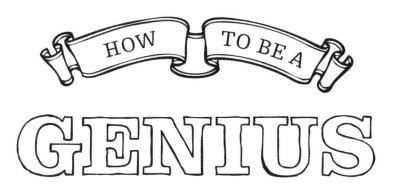

HOW TO BE A GENIUS

BRAIN TRAINING
FOR THE IDLE MINDED

Robert Allen

COLLINS & BROWN

CONTENTS

Introduction 6

CHAPTER 1:
IT'S ALL IN THE MIND...9
What is the Brain? 10
History of the Human Brain: A Timeline 13
Five Reasons Why Humans are Capable of Genius 15

CHAPTER 2:
BOOSTING YOUR BRAIN POWER 18
Brainteasers...19
Code Breaking 23
Puzzles 25
Pub Quizzes...31
Kakuro 34
Mind Games..37
Chess Challenges 39
Healthy Body and Mind 45
Boosting your Five Senses 47
Boosting your Ten Intelligences..50
Speed Reading 53
Mind Mapping 55

CHAPTER 3:
MIND CONTROL & CREATIVE THOUGHT 57
NLP..58
Relaxation 60
Basic Meditation...64
Advanced Meditation 66
Self Hypnosis...68
The Land of Nod...72

Lucid Dreams 74
Unconscious Incubation 76
Concentration 79
Creativity 83
Original Thought..90
Removing Thinking Blocks 94
Problem Solving..99
Lateral Thinking 101
Brainstorming 104
Under Pressure 108
Creativity from Confusion 110
Randomizing...112
Libido and Mortido 116
The Doors of Perception 118

CHAPTER 4:
MEMORY DEVELOPMENT TRICKS 121
Short Term Memory Tips...122
Long Term Memory Tips...127
Mnemonics 134
Ritual 136
Musical Memories 139
Revision Techniques 141
Visualization 143
Rhythm and Rhyme..148
Kinaesthetics 150
Smell 151
Storytelling 153
Repetition 155
Physical Reminders...158
Eidetic Memory 159
Techniques for Better Recall.......................................160
Buzan's Top 99 Geniuses and their IQs 162

Quiz Answers..164

INTRODUCTION

THE BRAIN.

Think about it.

Think about what it *actually* is.

Think about how on Earth it came to be in *your* head.
Now, think about how it works seamlessly without you
even needing to think about it.

And *think* about it.

Mind-boggling, isn't it?

The brain, your brain, has evolved to be one the most complex, beautiful and mysterious machines in the universe – its power is unparalleled even by today's super-powered computers. It is, quite simply, the greatest living thing any human being has ever – *will ever* – possess.

And yet, despite how amazing it is, it often gets overlooked. Perhaps considered not as cool as other appendages or organs the body has. It gets taken for granted even though it does millions of different things at once. As chaotic as it is disciplined, your brain never stops working even when the body has long given up; the brain, at night, storing the days events, cataloguing it, archiving it, for use at a later date. You don't hear it, or feel it or think about it doing these things … it just does them for you. But if you want a picture of what happened, let's say last Thursday at 11am, think about it …... and there it is. *In your head.* You can visualise that moment instantly. You can actually be back there in your own mind.

HOW?

Well, that's what the point of this book. To learn solely about your brain, and how you can use it to maximum effect. Because, let's face it, you probably aren't. With the increase in usage of different forms of modern multimedia as well as the recent influx of brain-training computer games on portable devices, it is believed that we are all getting smarter. But we are not. A recent study has shown that brain-training computer games are no better for you brain than browsing the web – and just browsing the web isn't always good for your mind. Indeed, all these new types of technology – from computer games, the internet to social networking – are actually rewiring our brains. All this technology is actually changing the way we think. A report by Ofcom in 2010 revealed that almost 50% of an adult's waking hours is used up by watching TV, the internet or on a mobile phone. That's an awful lot of time! There are no current studies to suggest that all this new technology and entertainment is harmful to our brains and health but it does distract us from putting our brains to better use. In 2010 it was even detailed in a BBC report that people with busy social lives have larger amygdalas – the part of the brain that is commonly linked with emotional health and mental well-being – showing that connections between how the brain interacts with the world and its overall health and development is something to be mindful of, particularly for younger children in this predominantly media-based age.

So, this book is not a rallying call for the pre-TV days – far from it – or to dis-invent some of mankind's most recent wonderful technological innovations so that humans can focus more on increasing brainpower rather than distracting it. But it is a call to have a think about your brain and how you choose to use it and for what purpose. The brain isn't just something that should sit in your head and do nothing. It should be challenged, it *wants* to be challenged and the more you challenge it, the better it becomes and the more you can get out of it and it gets out of you. This book, with 50 ways to make you smarter, as well as lots of essential facts and details about the mind, will help you begin how to make the most of the grey matter in your head, not only so that it stays fighting fit in the future (who knows what you might need it for?) but also so that it works harder for you, so that you can do more, learn more and understand more of the world around you.

From combating stress to eating superfoods, learning mind-mapping to conquering chess, through to lucid dreaming and code breaking, this book will help inspire your brain much more uniquely than any gimmicky computer game – the entries and methods used in this book are real, expert-approved techniques to boosting brainpower. After all, history's wisest men were not celebrated for using the brain they were born with, they are celebrated for challenging it beyond the normal call of duty. And you too can do the same.

Now a word of warning: It's not all easy. None of the advice in this book is. In fact some of the tricks and tips will make your brain feels as if you've eaten too much ice cream. But that's not a bad thing sometimes.

So, let's get cracking.
Remember – you can achieve anything you want
as long as you put your mind to it.

Literally.

CHAPTER 1

IT'S ALL IN
THE MIND

'When a *true* genius appears in the world,
you may know him by this sign:
that the dunces are all in confederacy against him.'

Jonathan Swift, *Thoughts on Various Subjects* **(1711)**

WHAT IS THE BRAIN?

Our brain is the organ that controls and operates the nervous system of the human body. Made up of over 100,000,000,000 nerve cells, or neurons, the brain stores our memories, controls all our bodily functions and abilities, enables us to communicate and react to our surroundings, and above all, gives us the power to think with individual imagination.

Over several million years, human beings have evolved from primitive single celled organisms called prokaryotes to complex multi-cellular forms, before arriving at our current state of advanced Homo sapiens. This evolution has given us the chance to adapt, develop and become in control of our bodies and minds. It's not been a simple journey; it has been one rife with danger, trial and many errors.

Everything living is made up of cells. Just as a cell's nucleus – often referred to as the brain of cells – have developed and adapted over a series of millennia before humans even existed, so to has the human brain. Two hundred thousand years ago, when prehistoric Man learnt to command fire, as well as cooking the meat of animals (as opposed to eating it raw), the amount of blood used in our bodies to digest this meat was drastically reduced. This excess blood in our systems allowed, over time, the brain to adapt and to grow in size and speed, enabling humans to move, outwit and dominate other mammals. In time, we came to conquer the entire planet.

Over the past few centuries – as our intelligence has sharpened, along with advances in technology and medicine – many famous thinkers, scientists and doctors have tried to split the brain up into its component parts, either psychologically or biologically. What we know now is that the brain can be split up in two effective ways. The left side of our brain controls speech, writing and all the logical aspects of body functioning and processing body data. The right side of the brain works in a slightly different way, it acts more randomly, less disciplined. This side controls creativity, emotions and intuition. It's as if you have two brains in your head, that work as one.

REGIONS OF THE BRAIN

The human brain consists of several regions, each of which is responsible for activities necessary for life. These regions include the brainstem, cerebellum, limbic system, diencephalon, and cerebral cortex. The cerebral cortex – which makes up about 80 per cent of the brain – is further split into four lobes: frontal, parietal, temporal and occipital. These lobes are connected, and made up of, billions of neurons and glia. It is these neurons that do all the hard work of the brain, sending bursts of electrical signals from the cerebral cortex to around the body, making it move and work. The glia acts as a bodyguard for the neurons, protecting and nourishing them so they continue working.

While the brain's size is a good indication of intelligence in mammals, the most important aspect is the brain's size in relation to the body's weight. Our human brain weighs around 1.4kg (3lb) that, as a percentage of body weight, is the biggest brain on the planet at about 2 per cent of the body's overall weight. In comparison, a lion only has a brain that takes up 0.1 per cent of its overall weight. A human brain is 78 per cent water, 11 per cent lipids, 8 per cent protein and 1 per cent carbohydrate. If your brain was a modern day personal computer (which it is, in effect) then the storage space it would contain is estimated at 1000 terabytes. Pretty astonishing stuff.

LEFT   RIGHT

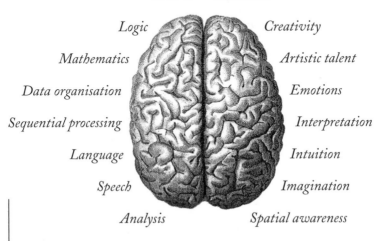

LEFT	RIGHT
Logic	Creativity
Mathematics	Artistic talent
Data organisation	Emotions
Sequential processing	Interpretation
Language	Intuition
Speech	Imagination
Analysis	Spatial awareness

BRAIN CONTROL

Everyday our fives senses are bombarded with stimuli that the brain must detect. For each stimulus a new connection within the brain is made and a unique electrical pulse is sent around the body. The brain processes the information the senses detect, before storing and memorising it, be it in our short term or long-term memory. We may not be able to recall every time we have ever scratched our head, but are potentially able to recall haircuts we had when we were young.

When we sleep, our brains tidy up the day's events – virtual housekeeping, if you will – storing the right items in the appropriate regions of the brain, ready for use another time. As human beings are predominantly visual creatures, the visual cortex of the brain has a lot of work to do, particularly as our eyes contain over 130,000,000 photoreceptors that are constantly active. Try and remember that the next time you walk into a crowded room!

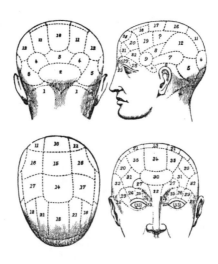

HISTORY OF THE HUMAN BRAIN: A TIMELINE

O ver the relatively recent period of human evolution, our brains have continued to grow larger and have continued to fit and adapt as the world around them has changed.

Here is a selected history of the human brain and its size:

PRE-AUSTRALOPITHECINE

6–7 million years ago
Sahelanthropus tchadensis
350 cubic centimetres (cc)

5.8–4.4 million years ago
Ardipithecus ramidus
400cc (chimp-size)

GENUS AUSTRALOPITHECUS

3.9–2.9 million years ago
Australopithecus afarensis
375–500cc

3–2 million years ago
Australopithecus africanus
500cc

2.1 – 1.1 million years ago
Australopithecus boisei
530cc

GENUS HOMO

2.4–1.5 million years ago
Homo habilis
500–800cc

1.8 million–300,000 years ago
Homo erectus
750–1225cc

780,000 years ago
Homo antecessor
1000cc

500,000 years ago
Homo heidelbergensis
1200cc

230,000–30,000 years ago
Homo neanderthalensis
1450cc

50,000–10,000 years ago
Cro-Magnon (Homo sapiens)
1350cc

195,000 years ago–today
Homo sapiens
1350cc

Weight
The weight of the human brain is about 3 lbs.

FIVE REASONS WHY HUMANS ARE CAPABLE OF GENIUS

C reativity is a human characteristic. And while recent reports suggest that creativity appears much like insanity in the way that brain in both sets of people lack receptors used to filter and direct thought, creativity is also what gives humans – all humans – genius-like capabilities. While other creatures possess many remarkable abilities – they can fly, run faster than us, hear better than us and have a much more developed sense of smell – they will never be able to learn to create in the very special way that humans do.

1. BOUNDLESS CURIOSITY

We are amazingly curious about the world around us. Cats may be a byword for curiosity, but the cat is a mere dullard when compared to even the stupidest of human. Humans want to know everything. We don't explore merely because it might help us to find extra food, or to defend our territory against enemies – we explore for the pure joy of it. We always want to know how things work, why things happen in the way they do and what lies over the horizon. This curiosity on its own would constitute a powerful weapon, but allied to other abilities, it turns into something truly amazing.

2. ABSTRACT THOUGHT

Humans have the ability to understand the abstract concepts. We can use ideas in a way that other species cannot. Even people who are not 'thinkers' have no trouble with concepts such as truth, justice or honesty. The power to deal in abstract ideas has led to some remarkable human achievements – for example Einstein's *Theory of Relativity*. Although most people have no idea what relativity is all about, it does not alter the fact that certain humans with a highly developed capacity for abstract thought are able to entertain ideas of astonishing complexity.

3. UNSTOPPABLE CREATIVITY

Creativity is a fundamental part of our nature. We constantly search for new ways to do things, and for new things to do. Take spiders, for example. They have been building webs in the same way for millions of years. Have any of them thought of turning the thing on its side and using it as a trampoline? Of course not. Have any of them considered that by twanging the threads it might possibly work as a musical instrument? Again, the answer is no. Would humans have had these thoughts? You bet! Humans are inventors and problem-solvers. We constantly try out new ideas just for the fun of it. Many of the ideas don't work, but that never bothers us because eventually we will find one that does.

Brain Speed
Information around the brain can be processed as quickly
as 268 miles per hour (120 meters/sec).

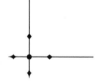

4. FAVOURABLE CONDITIONS

Animals struggle to live. They not only have to compete for food and shelter, but they mist also keep an eye out for predators. In the wild, the overwhelming majority don't even live long enough to reach sexual maturity. In prosperous countries, we live in a way that previous generations would have marvelled at. We have no predators, food is plentiful and homes are not too hard to come by. There are two main consequences that flow from this. Firstly, we have the luxury of being able to devote huge amounts of energy to matters that have no immediate survival value (art and literature, for example). Secondly, we increasingly live to a great age. Once our lives as parents are over, we are by no means a spent force and have many years of productive existence ahead of us.

5. CREATIVE SURGES

One of the most exciting facts about creativity is that it breeds more creativity. For example, we are constantly finding better and faster means to communicate with each other. Not so very long ago, communication was quite slow and inefficient – there were no computers, no mobile phones, and TV broadcasts were confined to the evenings. If you wanted to communicate with someone in another part of the country or overseas, you would probably write a letter. Nowadays, everyone keeps in touch by phone and the internet. In terms of creativity, this means that minds all over the world can be brought to focus on a single project with great ease. A team with members in, say, America, Australia, England, Italy and Japan can achieve an immediacy of communication, which is in itself the product of creative energy, is the means by which further creative leaps will take place.

CHAPTER 2

BOOSTING YOUR BRAIN POWER

'Playing mind sports
like chess or doing a crossword
can serve as a *gymnasium* for the *mind*
and keep you mentally fit.'

Raymond Keene, Chess Grandmaster

BRAINTEASERS

Brainteasers are a fun (if you can solve them!) way to stimulate or 'tease' your grey matter into life. They come in many forms – including lateral thinking, logic puzzles, visual puzzles and riddles – and they usually require unconventional thinking to solve them. Try some of these brainteasers for size. (Answers on p164).

BOUDICCA'S BIRTHDAY

AIM Here's a problem that will test your mathematical skills.

TASK Boudicca died 129 years after Cleopatra was born. If you add their ages at death together you get 100. Cleopatra died in 30 BC. So when was Boudicca born?

DEAR DEPARTED

AIM This is a rather tricky logic puzzle based on an actual epitaph dating from 1538. See if you can work out the relationships involved.

TASK

Two grandmothers with their two granddaughters,
Two husbands with their two wives,
Two fathers with their two daughters,
Two mothers with their two sons,
Two maidens with their two mothers,
Two sisters with their two brothers,
Yet only six lie buried here,
All born legitimate, from incest clear.

WHAT'S IN A NAME?

AIM This is a simple test for your verbal reasoning ability.

TASK What do the following words have in common?

ARMY   TEAK   YACHT   HURT   SAIL

Doing the task Many word puzzles depend on anagrams. It's always worth checking to see whether the words supplied can be rearranged in some meaningful way.

FOUR SQUARE

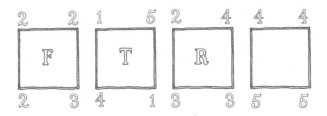

AIM This is a test of logical thinking. It requires only primary maths but, even so, will prove tricky for some.

TASK Look at the four squares. What letter should go in the centre of the square on the right?

CROSS QUIZ

AIM This is really a straightforward piece of logic if you don't let yourself be scared off by the wording.

TASK John is now just one and a third times as old as he was when he built his house and little Ben, who was 3? years old when John built the house, is now two years more than half as old as John's wife, Kate, was when John built the house, so that when little Ben is as old as John was when he built the house, their three ages combined will add up to 100 years. How old is Ben?

DAY DISORDER

AIM This is purely an exercise in clear thinking. The problem is actually quite easy but the wording makes your brain ache.

TASK When the day before yesterday was referred to as 'the day after tomorrow', the day that was then called 'yesterday' was as far away from the day we now call 'tomorrow' as yesterday is from the day on which we shall now be able to speak of last Monday as 'a week ago yesterday'. What day is it?

> **HELP!**
> If you have trouble doing this in your
> head try drawing a time line.

FIFTEEN SQUARED

AIM This is quite a tricky little numerical problem. Trial and error will, eventually, give a solution but those with a talent for mathematical thinking should be able to get there by a more intuitive route.

TASK Here are the numbers from one to nine positioned in a three-by-three square.

$$1 \quad 2 \quad 3$$
$$4 \quad 5 \quad 6$$
$$7 \quad 8 \quad 9$$

Your job is to rearrange them so that each row, column and diagonal adds up to 15.

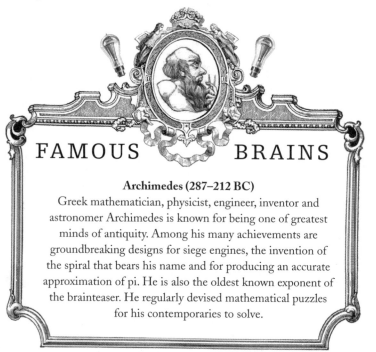

FAMOUS BRAINS

Archimedes (287–212 BC)
Greek mathematician, physicist, engineer, inventor and astronomer Archimedes is known for being one of greatest minds of antiquity. Among his many achievements are groundbreaking designs for siege engines, the invention of the spiral that bears his name and for producing an accurate approximation of pi. He is also the oldest known exponent of the brainteaser. He regularly devised mathematical puzzles for his contemporaries to solve.

CODE BREAKING

At its most sophisticated, code breaking (or cryptanalysis) utilizes advanced computer programs to decipher secret meanings and access encrypted data. Certainly, the world of cryptanalysis has moved on apace since the Colossus machines used by the British military to break German codes in World War II. But, at its simplest, code breaking is also a great way to boost your brain power. See if you can bust the code of these three teasers. (Answers on p165)

CODE BREAKER 1

AIM Most of the tasks concerned with communication are about improving your ability in this area, but a few are about defeating obstacles that hinder communication.

TASK Below you will find a message in code. Your task is to crack it. The code in question was invented by a secret society called the Rosicrucians and for centuries it remained secure. Even now, if you weren't given some help, you might find it too hard to crack. So look at the two diagrams below the code. They play a vital part in cracking it. Here's the message:

CODE BREAKER 2

AIM Here is a communications test based on your ability to decode a secret message. This offers you less help than the previous codes.

TASK The message below is in what is known as the Telephone Code. The diagram gives you a clue and, just to help you out, the answer is a song title. How quickly can you work it out?

3, 3, 8, 2, 6, 2, 1, 1, 2, 1, 1, 3, 1, 5, 1, 2

CODE BREAKER 3

AIM Here is a simple communications exercise based on a secret code. This will test your ingenuity.

TASK Here is a message in code:

E2.A5.E2B4D3B3.E4.C4.D5.A1.C2.A5.
D2.D2.E4.A3.B3.D2.B4.D3.C2.A1.D3.

How quickly can you decode it? Below is a hint to get you started. If you are really sharp you won't need to work out the whole message before you can guess the rest.

> **HELP!**
> This is mainly about context, both in terms of
> how the grid works and what the message contains.

PUZZLES

A puzzle is simply a problem which tests the ingenuity of the solver. Puzzles can be physical, such as the Rubik's Cube, which was a worldwide phenomenon in the 1980s, or a jigsaw puzzle. Yet they can also be logical, mathematical or word-based. Following on from the brainteasers on page 21, here are some puzzles to warm up your grey matter for the journey ahead. All answers are on pages 164-166.

PARTS PROBLEM

AIM There is no time in this test to use any reasoning powers, so you must rely solely on the acuity of your visual judgment.

TASK All you have to do is glance at the diagrams below for only five seconds and then decide which two figures contain the greatest number of segments.

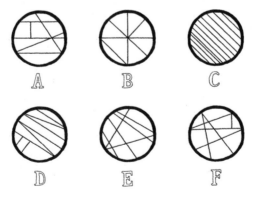

MISFIT

AIM Recognizing categories is an important mental ability. When we see something new for the first time we perform an instant sorting programme that tells us whether we can eat it, write with it or put it on the wall as a decoration, etc. Because we have a huge library of categories built up over years of experience, the process is usually instantaneous and we are not even aware of it. But what happens when you don't know what categories to use? Try this puzzle and find out.

TASK These words may appear to be quite unrelated but they have something in common. When you work out what it is you will be able to spot the one that doesn't fit.

APRIL HOLLY CHARITY DANDELION SANDY INDIA

FLAG FIGURE

AIM This is just a simple test of logic, but quite easy to get wrong.

TASK The Olympic flag bears five rings as shown:

How many ways are there of arranging the five rings?

LETTER PAIRS

AIM Is this really a word puzzle, a number puzzle or something quite different? The whole art of solving problems depends on recognizing what the problem is all about. Usually, once your mind is on the same wavelength as the person setting the puzzle, the answer is not that far away.

TASK Look at the following pairs. They all have something in common except for one. Which pair is the odd one out and why?

HR   AF   XS   MR   KF

NINES

AIM Here is a set of apparently random letters. How do you bring order to this confusion? Are they to be used as numbers, as parts of an anagram or do they have some other hidden significance? Once again, when you have unravelled the clue you should find the puzzle easy.

TASK Look carefully at the three-by-three letter grid. You will see that one of the letters is missing. There is a clue to help you: So to speak. When you discover what this is all about it should be obvious which letter you need to complete the grid.

E	R	A
P	T	N
S	E	?

TRANSPLANTATION

Here is a cunning little problem that will take a bit of sorting out. The picture shows an orchard of twenty-two trees. The owner wants to form twenty rows of four trees by transplanting six of the trees.

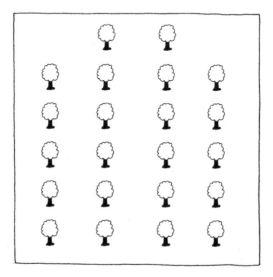

DELINQUENT DRIVER

AIM This sort of puzzle lures you into making false assumptions. All the information given is true but following the art of the politician, the story has been handled with 'economy'. Can you see where the lie lies?

TASK Four young men were going out for the day by car. As they were going through a town the driver jumped a red light and crashed into an oncoming vehicle injuring its driver badly. All the occupants of the men's car escaped unhurt. Although it was clearly the driver's fault and there were plenty of witnesses about, none of the four men were prosecuted. Why not?

FAMOUS BRAINS

Socrates (c.469BC–399BC)

Often hailed as the 'thinker's thinker' Socrates is the classical Greek philosopher whose teachings were the foundation that influenced other classical philosophers. Though Socrates never wrote any of his own texts (Plato did much of the word-spreading) he is known for his logic, sense of ethics and epistemology, such thoughts were considered highly advanced at the time. Indeed, through Plato and other thinkers who chronicled his life and his teachings, Socrates' work forms the basis of modern Western philosophy and his original teachings were passed down a veritable who-who's lineage of Greek thinkers: Socrates' student was Plato. Plato taught Aristotle who, in turn, went on to tutor Alexander the Great. Socrates was the father of them all though and, you could argue, the father of modern philosophy.

PRIZED POSSESSION?

AIM Lateral-thinking puzzles work by giving you incomplete or misleading information. To solve the puzzle you need to read the wording very carefully and then look for the holes in what it tells you. This one overlooks one very basic fact. As soon as you know what that is, the answer becomes obvious.

TASK You buy it, though you don't really want one. If you can't afford to buy it, you get given one. It protects you even though you don't need protection. It often continues working long after it's been disposed of. What is it?

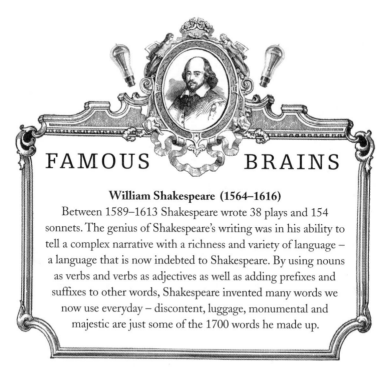

FAMOUS BRAINS

William Shakespeare (1564–1616)

Between 1589–1613 Shakespeare wrote 38 plays and 154 sonnets. The genius of Shakespeare's writing was in his ability to tell a complex narrative with a richness and variety of language – a language that is now indebted to Shakespeare. By using nouns as verbs and verbs as adjectives as well as adding prefixes and suffixes to other words, Shakespeare invented many words we now use everyday – discontent, luggage, monumental and majestic are just some of the 1700 words he made up.

PUB QUIZZES

The local pub quiz has become something of a social institution for many people in recent years. It's an excellent way to boost your knowledge and your memory in a relaxed surrounding with friends. The subject matters are often quite varied and however intelligent you might think you are, you will always discover some facts you didn't know. So if the pub quiz isn't already part of your weekly brain training regime, then ensure you remedy that as soon as possible.

And if you don't like going to pubs, there are many other ways of taking part in quizzes. For instance, play along during episodes of the worldwide television hit quiz, *Who Wants To Be A Millionaire?* or play quiz-related board games such as Trivial Pursuit.

Try the two quizzes below and then refer to p168 to see how many you got right. Why not devise your own quiz – you'll be amazed how much you'll learn by just researching a set of questions.

QUIZ 1

1. How many dots are there on a pair of dice?
2. How many stars are on the European Union flag?
3. Rather than a hatter, what is the proper name for a maker of hats?
4. What is the name of the poker hand containing three of a kind and a pair?
5. Astrologically speaking, two of the fire signs are Leo and Aries. Which is the third?
6. Who is said to rule in a Plutocracy?
7. What did Dr John S. Pemberton concoct in his backyard in 1886?
8. Who made the first telephone call to the moon?
9. In what year was the "Gunfight at the OK Corral"?
10. What is the capital of Iran?
11. In which country is Timbuktu?
12. By what name is Edson Arantes do Nascimento better known?
13. What is the highest-achievable break in snooker?
14. In which organ of the body is insulin produced?

15. What is the speed of sound at sea level called?
16. What is Hypermetropia?
17. What is the more common term used to denote a temperature of nought degrees Kelvin?
18. What is the official language of Brazil?
19. What is thanatology the scientific study of?
20. In which year was dynamite invented?
21. What percentage of the world's population is contained in the United States?
22. What word means gradually getting louder and louder?
23. In which month is the French national holiday of Bastille Day?
24. In which ocean are the Canary Islands?
25. Which country produces 70% of the world's olive oil?
26. How many hearts does an octopus have?
27. If a creature is edentulous what has it not got?
28. How is the number 14 written in Roman numerals?

QUIZ 2

A. How many prime numbers are there between 10 and 20?
B. What word is used to describe an angle between 90 and 180 degrees?
C. What is the next number in the sequence (1, 1, 2, 3, 5, 8,)?
D. What is the name given to the imaginary line of 180 degrees longitude?
E. How many milligrams are in one gram?
F. What will be the next year that reads the same upside down and back to front as it does the right way up?
G. Dendrology is the scientific study of what?

HELP!

Why would you buy it if you didn't want it? In what unusual circumstance might you buy something to protect you even if you didn't need protecting? How is it disposed of?

H. How many square feet are there in a square yard?
I. What does the acronym SCUBA stands for?
J. What's the next letter in this sequence 'OTTFFSSEN'?
K. What name is given to the 'halo' of gas that surrounds the sun?
L. What do you call the number below the line in a fraction?
M. What is 1999 in Roman numerals?
N. What does a horologist do?
O. How many land miles are there in a League?
P. How far can a sperm swim in an hour?
Q. What is the only rock that is edible to man?
R. What name is given to a female swan?
S. What is the square root of 169?
T. What unit is used to measure the frequency of radio waves?
U. Express 91 in Roman numerals.
V. What does the word dinosaur mean?
W. What is the epicarp of an orange?
X. What is the most common blood type in humans?
Y. How many pairs of chromosomes do humans have?
Z. What is the computer term Bit short for?

Answers to both quizzes on p166 – no cheating allowed.

KAKURO

Related to Soduko but often more challenging is the variant Kakuro, which is seen by many to be the mathematical version of the crossword.

Usually played in a 16x16 grid filled with black and white cells. Each part row or column contains either one number, or two (separated by a diagonal slash) commonly called 'clues'. The object of the puzzle is to insert a digit from 1 to 9 into each white cell such that the sum of the numbers in each entry matches the clue associated with it.

Once you've understood that it's time to tackle the puzzle. Below are 7 beginner level Kakuro's to start with – see if you can crack them.

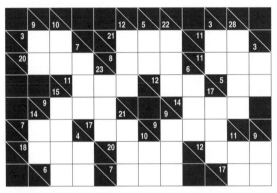

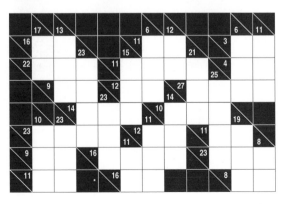

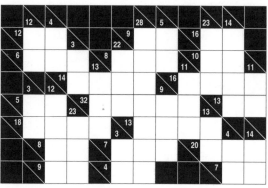

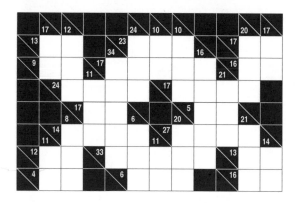

(Answers on p167)

ORIGIN OF NUMBER PUZZLES

Number puzzles such as Soduko and Kakuro are in fact nothing new.
Similar numerical teasers appeared in newspapers in late 19th century
France. Le Siècle, a Paris-based daily, published a partially completed
9x9 magic square with 3×3 sub-squares on November 19, 1892.

MIND GAMES

If you are asked to name a single mind game associated with geniuses, you would probably say 'chess'. And why not? It has a deserved reputation as a game of complex strategy and intellect and many of the world's greatest thinkers have excelled at it. But chess certainly isn't the only board game that can help turn you into a genius. You will find all of the pursuits described below helpful in your quest for sharper intellect and better recall. Read on.

CHESS

Chess is played on a chequered board with an 8x8 grid, with a total of 64 squares. Each player starts the game with 16 pieces comprised of: a single king and queen, a pair of rooks, knights and bishops, and eight pawns. The aim of the game is to 'checkmate' (trap) the opponent's king. It's the ultimate game of skill. Top protagonists can battle for many hours in a single game.

BACKGAMMON

Backgammon has a history stretching back 5,000 years and was played widely in the Middle East and Ancient Rome. Played with checkers and dice, the board is divided into two halves of 12 long triangles, called points. With each roll of the dice the player moves his or her checkers between the points, the object being to remove (bear off) all your checkers before your opponent can do the same. Although luck is certainly involved, strategic thinking plays a large part.

BRIDGE

Bridge is a card game played by four players (two competing pairs). Each player is dealt 13 cards. Each team has to bid for the number of 'tricks' (units of play) they think they will win based on the nominated trump. At the end of the 13 tricks points are awarded depending on the number of tricks won, against those bid for. It's a very good game to promote tactical awareness and improve your memory.

SCRABBLE

This is a word-based board game that is very useful for extending your vocabulary and improving your spelling. Players accumulate points by forming words from individually lettered and numbered titles on a 15x15 grid. Words can be laid on the grid horizontally or vertically and must join or bisect a word already on the grid.

DRAUGHTS

Draughts (or checkers as it's known in the United States) is thought to Ancient Egypt. It is played on either a 10x10 (or 8x8 – UK and US) light and dark chequered board. Each player starts with 20 (or 12) 'draughtsmen' which are only allowed to move on the dark squares. The object is to capture all the opponent's pieces by hopping them diagonally.

OTHERS TO TRY
Other games which promote strategy and skill include cribbage, various forms of poker and the Japanese chess game, Shogi.

CHESS CHALLENGES

I f you think of chess as a boring game for boffins, you may be pleasantly surprised by the variations described in this section. This book is regrettably too short to be able to enter into an explanation of the rules of the game, but as long as you can play a basic game of chess at beginner level, here are some great opportunities for you to think creatively.

If, on the other hand, you are a serious chess player, don't be too quick to dismiss these games as not worthy of your attention. They may not be chess as you know it, but they do provide interesting challenges that will bring the real rewards in terms of boosting your creative powers.

HIGH SPEED CHESS

- This game is played exactly like the normal game with one important exception: you get only 5 seconds to make your move!
- This game deprives players of the opportunity to indulge in long analyses of the game and forces quick decisions based largely on intuition.
- The results are always interesting, and experience chess players often find themselves at the mercy of less skills but quicker thinking and the series.
- The winner is the player who can call 'Checkmate'.

LOSING CHESS

- The object of this game is simply to you lose all your pieces.
- In this game, the king has no special status and can be taken just like any other piece.
- A player who is able to take a piece must do so. The first player to get rid of all his pieces is the winner.

REFUSAL CHESS

- This is just like the normal chess except that at each move, a player has the right to refuse the move of his adversary and insist that he plays some other move.
- The right of refusal may be exercised as many times as one likes during the game, but only one refusal is permitted per move.

KNIGHT ERRANT CHESS

- This is played just like normal chess, except that data player has an extra knight at his disposal.
- At any point during the game, the player whose turn it is may place his extra knight on any vacant square on the board. This counts as his move.
- After the knight has been placed, it simply continues to function like a normal knight.
- As you only get one chance to place your extra knight, the skill comes in deciding at which point in the game it will do you the most good.

DOUBLE JEOPARDY CHESS

- This is played like the normal game except that each player gets two moves at a time.
- A player who gives check on his first move must forfeit his second move.
- A player who is in check must use his first move to get out of check.

GENIUS CHESS

- This version really sorts out the heavyweight thinkers from the rest. You will need to cultivate an almost superhuman ability to think ahead.
- White starts with the usual one move.
- Black then gets two moves.
- White has three moves.
- Black has four moves, etc.
- When a player gives check this ends his turn and he forfeits the rest of his moves.
- A player who is in check must get out of check on his first move.

RANDOM CHESS

Random chess is just like normal chess except that actually beginning of the game, the pieces on the first rank are arranged in a random manner (which must be the same for both players). So, for example, you could have king, rook, bishop, queen, bishop, rook,knight, knight. This does strange and terrible things, especially to the opening of the game.

AND FINALLY

Why not try inventing a completely new game using a standard chess set? The object of the game and the moves of the pieces can all be altered to suit you. Who knows, you might end up producing the next craze to sweep the games market.

HEALTHY BODY
AND HEALTHY MIND

EATING AND DRINKING

For your memory to work properly, you need to look after yourself. It's no good assuming that you can put your mind to work whenever you want and despite the way you have treated yourself. Remember that your body and your mind are one. There are four main rules to maintaining a healthy body and mind: eating, drinking, exercise and sleep. Let's deal with your diet first.

EAT SENSIBLY

A good diet is essential to mental and physical health. Junk food is called that for a reason. Try to eat lots of fresh fruit and vegetables. There is no specific brain food, but eating lots of pizzas, burgers and takeaways will do dreadful things not just to your memory but to your general health. One thing is very important: eat breakfast! Researchers have found that those who eat breakfast have better powers of recall than those who don't.

Balanced diet
We need a balanced diet comprised of:
* **Proteins** – these break down during digestion to create chemicals which act as neurotransmitters.
* **Carbohydrates** – such as potatoes, pasta and sugar give a quick burst of energy
* **Fats** – the body needs fats to keep neural networks healthy. These are good for your memory.
* **Salts** are essential for all human cells to function, but need to be the right balance of sodium and potassium.
* **Fibre and vitamins** also play essential roles in keeping us healthy.

Little and often

Rather than eating one or two very large meals per day which makes us feel sleepy because the body requires extra bloody to aid digestion, it is recommended by nutritionists that you eat little and often. This method allows the whole body to receive a steadier supply of oxygenated blood and so the brain maintains a more constant state of alertness and high energy levels.

DRINKING HABITS

Alcohol

If you have never woken up in the morning unable to remember the events of the previous evening because you were a tad too enthusiastic with your drinking, I congratulate you. Most of us have done it at one time or another and you don't need me to tell you that it's a bad idea. If you want your memory to work well, booze is a very bad idea indeed, as are all drugs (including nicotine). For some of us, alcohol causes us to be less inhibited and so may improve our creativity, but as alcohol is a depressant it also reduces the flow of blood to the brain and so reduces thinking power. An occasional indiscretion will produce a mere memory blip, but long-term abuse can mess up your mind in various unpleasant ways. Loss of memory will almost certainly be one of them.

Caffeine

Caffeine is a double-edged sword. As a stimulant it can increase alertness in the short term, but, as it is a diuretic, it also leads to dehydration.

Water intake

Drinking plenty of water (at least two litres (4½ US pints) daily will help you stay hydrated. Dehydration in humans means that your brain functions at less than full capacity. This is fact. It has been proved that children who drink eight glasses of water a day do better in test results than those drinking mostly sugar-based drinks.

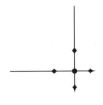

FAMOUS BRAINS

Albert Einstein (1879–1955)

Albert Einstein – with his characteristic white hair and humble background – was a man who simply revolutionized the world. His *General* and *Special Theories of Relativity* of 1916, built on Isaac Newton's notion of gravity, and took it to an even more advanced level of quantum theory. It was discovered after his death that Einstein's *corpus callosum* – the part of the brain that connects the left and right hemispheres – was larger than your average man. This, in part, would have helped in Einstein's intellectual and scientific thinking – the natural ability to powerfully connect the right, intuitive part of the brain to the left, logical part.

HEALTHY BODY AND HEALTHY MIND

EXERCISE AND SLEEP

Just as important as eating and drinking sensibly is physical activity and rest. Exercise clears the mind and stimulates endorphins. While sleep allows the brain and the body to recuperate after the stresses and strains of the day.

GET EXERCISE

Any form of aerobic exercise is good for you. During exercise your brain is given the message that more oxygen is required. As a result the body produces more red blood cells, containing more oxygen. An aerobically fit person can produce twice as much oxygen at any given time as an unfit person. Oxygen of course is the ultimate energy source your brain needs for 'thinking.

You don't have to live at the gym, but you do need a certain amount of exercise for your mind and body to function at maximum efficiency. Walking the dog (briskly) or mowing the lawn will do just as well, if you hate sports. But why not put in a little bit of extra effort and go for a long walk, or a swim? The dividends in both the long and short-term are well worth the input.

There are of course many forms of exercise that you can choose, from the relatively sedate (pilates and golf) to the highly strenuous (triathlon). Experiment with different types of exercise until you find something that suits you, and if possible find someone to do it with. The worry about letting the other person down might act as an added incentive to keep going. And schedule that exercise into your diary, just as you do an evening out with friends.

GET ENOUGH SLEEP

As adults we need an average of eight hours sleep a night. Over time, lack of sleep can lead to poor concentration (reducing your ability to learn), low energy and mood swings. Without enough sleep our brains do not function at their full capacity.

The quality of sleep is actually more important than the quantity, however. A person who has had four of five hours' unbroken sleep – former Prime Minister Margaret Thatcher famously took only four hours sleep a night – will often feel more recuperated than someone who has had a restless sleep for 10 hours.

During periods of deep sleep, or REM (Rapid Eye Movement), your brain processes all that has happened during the day. The particular neurotransmitter which is produced during REM helps keep neural networks healthy and this actually improves the memory-forming process.

First sense

The first sense to develop while in your mother's wombe is the sense of touch. The lips and cheeks can experience touch at about 8 weeks and the rest of the body around 12 weeks.

SNACK BEFORE BEDTIME

Eating a large meal shortly before bedtime is a bad idea. However, eating a non-sugary snack, such as a banana which contains a natural sedative, might be beneficial – it's now known that a drop in blood-sugar levels during the night is a common cause of sleep disruption.

BOOSTING YOUR FIVE SENSES

You might assume that there is very little correlation between the senses of sight, sound, touch, smell and touch – and your intelligence. But there is strong evidence to suggest that the better you use your five senses the more efficiently your brain will perform. The following activities are designed to make you more aware of your senses.

SMELL

Smells are very useful at evoking powerful memories and feelings, as we will discover on pxx, because every time we breathe in, the odours we inhale come into contact with the nerves in our noses. And these nerves are directly in contact with the brain's emotion processing area. The nose contains five million receptors and most people can detect only 10,000 odours.

Boost your smell

Test the power of smell to give rise to emotions by visiting a food market. As you walk around literally breathing in the atmosphere, identify five different smells. What thoughts and feelings do you associate with each smell?

Supertasters
There is a class of people known as supertasters who not only have more taste buds on the tongue, but whose brain is more sensitive to the tastes of foods and drinks. In fact, they can detect some flavors that others cannot.

SIGHT

Our eyes are incredible. They contain 130 million photoreceptors which enable us to distinguish millions of colours and hundreds of shades of brightness, as well as size, perspective, distance, shape and movement.

Boost your sight

Sit in a chair facing out of the window and focus on an object in your field of vision. Write down the shape and size of the object. Which and how many colours is it formed of? If it is a sunny day, do the shadows have an affect? View the object through first your left eye only and then your right eye only. Has viewing the object in this way altered its appearance?

SOUND

The human ear is a complex tool made up of several parts. The outer ear direct sounds towards the tympanic membrane, which transmits vibrations to the cochlea (which contains 16,000 hair cells) through a series of small bones. The cochlea reacts to these vibrations and transmits impulses to the brain via the auditory nerve. The ear can perceive frequencies from 16 cycles per second, which is a very deep bass, to 28,000 cycles per second, which is a very high pitch. Bats and dolphins can detect frequencies higher than 100,000 cycles per second.

Boost your hearing

Sit quietly in a chair and spend three minutes listening to the sounds around you. Separate the sounds in your mind – some bird song, some distant music, a car. Which of the sounds are loud and which are quiet? Focus of those closest and then those in the distance. Then try to ignore these outside sounds and listen instead to the sound of your own breath and those in your body.

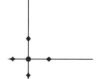

TOUCH

Our skin is the largest organ in our body. It measures about 21 square feet. Nerve endings in the skin and other parts of the body transmit sensations to the brain. Some parts of the body, like fingertips, have a larger number of nerve endings and, therefore, are more sensitive. The skin has 200,000 receptors for cold, 500,000 for contact and 2,800,000 for pain.

Boost your touch

Touch everything in your immediate vicinity. If you are sitting in your living room, the sofa, a cushion, the TV remote control, even this book. Let yourself become aware of everything you are touching, either directly or indirectly (even the seat pressing on your legs) are focus on how it feels.

TASTE

Human taste receptors, or taste buds, are situated mainly in the tongue. They are able to detect four basic tastes: salty (top and side of the tongue), sweet (the tip), bitter (back of the tongue), and sour (top and side of the tongue). There is also a fifth taste sensation, 'umami', detected by taste buds sensitive to amino acids. At the base of each taste bud there is a nerve that sends the sensations to the brain.

Boost your taste

Close your eyes and get a friend to give you a food you haven't eaten before or perhaps a food that you disliked as a child. Try to determine its taste and classify it as salty, sweet, bitter or sour by putting a little on the different parts of your tongue in turn.

BOOSTING YOUR 10 INTELLIGENCES

Psychologists and philosophers first attempted to categorise and assess the intelligence levels of human beings in the early 1900s. William Stern and Alfred Binet formulated tests designed to rate the intelligence levels of different people – or their Intelligence Quotient (IQ).

As with most aspects of research, on a range of topics, this study of intelligence has developed and improved over time. It is now accepted by many experts in the field that the IQ of human beings is comprised of 10 factors. The following text summarises those 10 factors and suggests ways in which you can improve your intelligence in each area.

1. MATHEMATICAL

DEFINITION: Excel at puzzles and logic problems such as those that appear earlier in this book. You are good at finding out how things work and ways to fix them and are likely to make numbered lists of tasks.

IMPROVE YOUR INTELLIGENCE BY: looking for numbers in everyday life. Create your own simple equations by, for instance, keeping a running total of the cost of items in your shopping trolley, or trying to understand how odd work in sports betting.

2. PRACTICAL

DEFINITION: Good at sorting out tasks, prioritising and problem solving.

IMPROVE YOUR INTELLIGENCE BY: copy the techniques used by a friend or family member who is known for their practical abilities and use them in situation you face.

3. VISUAL

DEFINITION: Good appreciation of textures, colours, shapes. Probably good at art.

IMPROVE YOUR INTELLIGENCE BY: using diagrams and pictures instead of words to describe a story or take notes at a forthcoming meeting.

4. PHYSICAL

DEFINITION: Good at any form of sport or physical activity. Often animated with hand gestures while talking.

IMPROVE YOUR INTELLIGENCE BY: Generally be more active – walk instead of taking the bus. Stretch and become better ware of the muscles in your body.

5. SOCIAL

DEFINITION: Comfortable in large groups; good at team building tasks and often takes the lead.

IMPROVE YOUR INTELLIGENCE BY: seeking out a relative stranger in your office or a familiar face from your street and engaging them in conversation.

6. EMOTIONAL

DEFINITION: In touch with your emotions and those of others. Not averse to self-improvement or counselling.

IMPROVE YOUR INTELLIGENCE BY: keeping a diary or journal. Honestly recall how you felt at certain parts of the day and how your behaviour affected others.

7. LINGUISTIC

DEFINITION: Good at spelling and grammar and possesses a wide vocabulary. Avid reader of books.

IMPROVE YOUR INTELLIGENCE BY: attempting word puzzles such as crosswords; find time to learn another language.

8. MUSICAL

DEFINITION: Interested in music and perhaps plays one or more instruments; has good rhythm and is able to keep a beat.

IMPROVE YOUR INTELLIGENCE BY: listening more intently to music. Try to identify the different instruments that go into producing the overall sound you can hear.

9. SPIRITUAL

DEFINITION: Not necessarily religious, but certainly interested in the fundamentals questions concerning life and our purpose on Earth.

IMPROVE YOUR INTELLIGENCE BY: Read up about the key beliefs inherent in the world's leading religions, especially those marginalised in your country of birth.

10. ENVIRONMENTAL

DEFINITION: Good understanding of flora and fauna and problems posed by climate change. Conscious of your carbon footprint.

IMPROVE YOUR INTELLIGENCE BY: appreciating the natural world around you. Next time you walk in the countryside, look at the plants animals you encounter, even the shape of clouds. Research anything with which you are unfamiliar when you return home.

SPEED READING

Speed reading is the term for a collection of techniques aimed at increasing the speed at which the eye can see and the brain can absorb information without any loss of comprehension.

From early school age many people are taught that speed reading is bad. For instance it is better to read slowly and carefully, reread sentences if you have not understood them and reads everything word-for-word. Yet these beliefs are untrue.

The human eye works like a camera. In order to register information it needs to fix on a subject for a fraction of a second before moving on. This is the case whether it is a picture on a television screen or a few words on the page of a book. Slow readers are able to fix on one or two words at a time; while speed readers can digest three to six words. Over the course of 60 seconds a slow reader might read 100 words, whereas a speed reader is capable of 1,000 words in that time. A good speed (or range) reader is also able to utilise his or her peripheral vision horizontally and vertically in addition to the central focus, which can increase the words per minute rate much farther still.

In order to digest the maximum information during any one visual fix the reader needs to develop what is known as the Cyclopean Perception. The lives and environment of people today often lead to them focusing the brain solely on whatever the eyes can see, a 'tunnel vision', if you will. But to become a good speed reader and therefore more intelligent, you need to use the 'central' eye of the brain itself (Cyclopean Perception) to sift through everything in its range of vision. The ability to achieve this has been a feature of all the greatest minds through history.

'Reading is to the mind
what *exercise* is to the body.'
Sir Richard Steele (1672–1729)

IMPROVED READING SPEED
= IMPROVED INTELLIGENCE

Try these eight tips to improve your reading speed and comprehension:

1. Absorb more words with each visual fix.
2. Increase the speed of each visual fix – do not dwell.
3. Focus only on the words on the page – do not become distracted.
4. Read important words or phrases out loud.
5. Be interested in, and positive about, what you are reading.
6. Maintain a good posture while reading
7. Always move your eyes forward on the page – never skip back to content.
8. Develop your Cyclopean Perception.

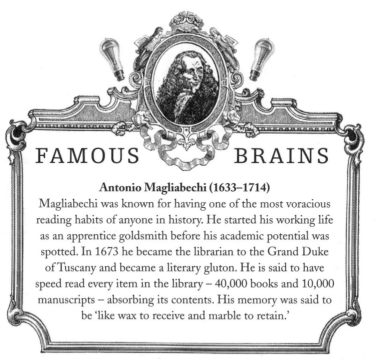

FAMOUS BRAINS

Antonio Magliabechi (1633–1714)

Magliabechi was known for having one of the most voracious reading habits of anyone in history. He started his working life as an apprentice goldsmith before his academic potential was spotted. In 1673 he became the librarian to the Grand Duke of Tuscany and became a literary gluton. He is said to have speed read every item in the library – 40,000 books and 10,000 manuscripts – absorbing its contents. His memory was said to be 'like wax to receive and marble to retain.'

MIND MAPPING

A mind map is a hand drawn diagram used as a creative or memory tool as an alternative to note-taking. It can feature words, pictures, ideas or tasks which branch off from a central concept or subject. Mind maps are useful for generating, classifying and structuring ideas and are often advocated as a studying tool and as a means of solving problems or making decisions.

Mind mapping stimulates your brain much more than traditional note-taking. The latter relies on just a few of the brain's cortical skills – with the use of words, lists and analysis. It's also very visually restricted, dealing in one colour – usually the black or blue of the pen or pencil you are using. Single colour or monotone is boring for the brain and when the brain becomes bored it 'tunes out'. You may have experienced this for yourself – daydreaming (or even falling asleep) while making lists for exam study or while note-taking during lectures at university.

Mind mapping, in contrast, makes extensive use of colours. The act of producing a mind map stimulates the right side of the brain (containing artistic ability, creativity and imagination, among others) and well as the left side. It's also superior than note-taking because it saves time – you focus on key words and images rather than superfluous content in a list; and it's proven to increase you memory capacity.

HOW TO MIND MAP

Follow these basic rules to produce your first mind map. Always refer back to them to ensure you maximise the potential of using this technique.

1. **CENTRAL IMAGE.** Always start with an image containing at least three colours. For the sake of this example let's say you are producing a mind map on the city of Paris. Your central image could be something iconic such as the Eiffel Tower.
2. **CLARITY AND VARIETY.** Images can be as simple or as complicated as you like, depending on your artistic skills, and should vary in size and texture. Certainly don't be disheartened if you think you cannot draw well.

3. **ORDER OF IMPORTANCE.** Branch out from the central image with different thought and subject strands, then split these into sub-sections, compiled in order of importance. For our Paris example these initial subjects could comprise architecture, food, wine, culture, sport etc.
4. **KEY WORDS.** Limit the text on your map to short key words, a maximum of two or three for each branch or line.
5. **LINE THICKNESS.** These should reflect the importance of the subjects; the more important, the thicker the line.
6. **SPACING.** If you are struggling to complete a particular section of your map, leave a space for it and return to it later.
7. **CONNECTING LINES.** Use symbols curves, arrows or whichever codes you deem to be appropriate to link the lines together and bring cohesion to you map. It needs to flow in a way that's logical to your thoughts processes.
8. **THE FIVE SENSES.** Uses images and words that relate to sight, smell, sound, taste and touch. This will help your memory. For instance, if you are fond of the French dish, coq au vin, write it down. It will stimulate your sense of smell and taste buds for better recall of the Food section of you map.

You will find it easier and more productive to mind map effectively if you are positive, you free your mind of cluttered thoughts, sit in a comfortable environment and work in natural light. Good luck.

ORIGINS OF MIND MAPPING

Although list making has held sway as a method of recording thoughts and ideas throughout time, the graphic record of the mind map is certainly not a 21st century phenomenon. Some of the earliest examples were developed by the Ancient Greek philosopher Porphyry of Tyros (234–305 AD). He is known to have produced an early version of the mind map as he sought to better comprehend the work of Aristotle. A thousand years later another philosopher, the Spaniard Ramon Llull (1235–1315), was also an advocate of these techniques.

CHAPTER 3

MIND CONTROL & CREATIVE THOUGHT

'*Creative thinking* may mean simply
the realisation that there is no particular virtue
in doing things the way they have
always been done.'

Rudolph Flesch, philosopher

NLP

Have you ever thought that you could not learn something? Have you ever found that your brain closed down when you were under stress? Do you have difficulty in solving problems? Has your communication ever been misunderstood? Do you procrastinate when faced with a difficult situation? If your answer to these questions is 'yes', then NLP could help.

The concept of Neuro-Linguistic Programming is unbelievably simple: it applies objectivity (which is the way we really think, because we are humans, rather than robots). NLP began in the early 1970s as a twinkle in the eye of a mathematician and computer wizard called Richard Bandler who was interested in therapy. While he was a student at the University of California in Santa Cruz, he joined forces with John Grinder, Professor of Linguistics at the UC, and the two of them worked together to put NLP on the map.

NLP has been described as the study of the structure of subjective experience: how the way we process our thoughts affects our internal experience; how our internal experience affects our behaviour; and how our behaviour affects everyone else. NLP is a way of thinking about thinking. It is about how we know things. How do you know that you like spending time with one person rather than with another? How do you know that you cannot learn something? How do you know that you want to read this book? What process inside you gives you your information?

The name, Neuro-Linguistic Programming, describes the components of this combination of art and techniques.

NEURO: information is stored in our nervous system, which reacts in one way or another to every situation, for example, scientists have measured over 1,500 different neurological responses to stress.

LINGUISTIC: the language that we use demonstrates, at a deep subconscious level, what is going on inside us; for example, if I ask you to look at something from my point of view, I am processing my thoughts in pictures, and inviting you to do the same; if you reply that we are getting bogged down with detail, I will realize that you are not into pictures at the moment – you are processing through your feelings, and your feelings are that we are not getting anywhere very fast.

PROGRAMMING: in order to save time and effort in checking out each piece of information that we receive, we run automatic programmes, for example, we see a red light and we stop, without thinking; someone smiles at us, and we smile back. Some of us run programmes that are out of date: we may panic when we see a spider, or are asked to take a test or make a speech, or if someone mentions mathematics; we may die a thousand deaths if we make a mistake, or if somebody laughs at us. And one of the questions that NLP asks is: are these programmes still useful, or would we rather have choices in how we react?

NLP is the study of excellence: what is the difference that makes the difference between someone who does something with ease, elegance and excellence, and someone who does not?

NLP gives you the chance to rediscover all those important things that you have always known at a very deep level, but which may have been considered frivolous or stupid by your 'elders and betters'. It is a study of the natural process of learning, and how and why we do it; it is also a study of the much more difficult process of 'not learning' and how and why we manage to do that.

RELAXATION

When your mind becomes stressed it starts to race, unable to concentrate on tasks at hand. Relaxation exercises are a great way to switch off your mind and let it recuperate.

INSTANT RELAXATION

AIM You can do this exercise anywhere – in the office, in the car (don't close your eyes!), even waiting in the last moments before an interview. It will also help you at times of sudden stress such as when you suddenly get some very bad news or discover that you've forgotten an important appointment and your boss is going to yell at you. This is not a substitute for deep relaxation but it's a good emergency measure that will help you to compose yourself in those moments of crisis.

TASK Take a slow, deep breath. Imagine your body is the top of an elevator shaft and that the air is going in through your nose and then right down to the centre of the Earth. Feel the air going down, and down, and down as you breathe in all the way.

– Hold your breath for three seconds.
– As you let the breath out, count slowly to five.
– Keep this up for about 10 minutes or until your panic subsides.

DOING THE TASK

Let your breathing settle into a nice, comfortable rhythm like the ebb and flow of the tide. Relaxation will come quickly but DON'T use this exercise to relax you so deeply that you fall asleep. When you hold your breath for three seconds, try not to let it become a strain because that will defeat the object. Hold the breath for a shorter time if that helps.

MOOD MANAGEMENT

AIM Like most people, you probably take your mood for granted. Why? All you ever know is your mind. There is no outside to the mind so even your body is just a mind object. Mood is a function of that mind and it is changeable by an act of will on your part. Do you ever start the day by getting yourself in the right mood, or do you just accept that you'll feel grotty on Monday morning and pretty good on Friday? This exercise will help you adjust your mood.

TASK This exercise is most suitable for early morning. Start by getting comfortable. It is especially important that you should be warm, but not too hot. You can lie in bed, or sit on a comfortable chair if you prefer. Try a few repetitions of the Instant Relaxation exercise on page 62. When you feel relaxed, start to concentrate on the mood you want to create. A little background music will help. Think of the positive aspects of the day ahead. Think of all the things you will enjoy during the day. Have a look at your world through rose-tinted glasses and see all that is good about your life. If you have worries, try to picture them written down on sheets of paper. Mentally pick up each sheet, rip it up and throw it away. As you do this, assure yourself that you can deal with all your problems. Tell yourself that you are full of courage and confidence and that nothing that happens during the day will faze you. Think about friends, colleagues (the ones you like) and loved ones, in fact anyone whose help and support makes your life more enjoyable. Your day should now start with you in a happy, relaxed and confident mood.

HELP
We tend to take the mind for granted, a bit like the weather.
It is important to get into the habit of believing that,
just as you can redecorate your room just as you like,
you also have power to adjust the set of your mind.

DEEP RELAXATION

AIM This is a very simple but powerful technique for recharging your batteries. You may think that the end result (going to sleep) is easily achieved without any special help, but the sleep you gain by this method will be deeper and far more relaxing than any sleep you've ever had before. It will refresh you thoroughly, reduce your stress levels and make you ready for whatever tasks lie ahead.

TASK Lie flat with a pillow under your head and your arms by your sides. Close your eyes and start to breathe slowly and deeply.

1) As you breathe in, let your stomach expand. On the out breath your stomach goes in.
2) Hold each inhalation for three seconds.
3) As you breathe out count to five slowly.

Repeat this step. Let your toes go completely relaxed.
Now start with your toes and scrunch them up tight. Then let them relax.
Repeat this step.

Now move on to your feet. Bend them forwards as though you were a ballet dancer about to dance on the points of your toes. Now relax.

Move slowly up your body alternately tensing and relaxing each set of muscles. Each group should be tensed and relaxed twice. Work in this order: toes, feet, calves, thighs, buttocks, stomach, back, arms, hands, neck, face, scalp.

> ### DOING THE TASK
> If you find it hard to let go, don't give up. People who find it
> difficult to relax are the ones who need to let go the most.
> Just go through the ritual regularly until you find it works.
> Very few people, except those racked with anxiety,
> can resist this method of relaxation.

MAGIC CARPET

AIM This is a form of relaxation guaranteed to produce a deep sleep and, very often, sweet dreams. It is useful for people suffering from stress.

TASK Start by lying on your bed. Make sure you are warm and comfortable and then carry out the Instant Relaxation exercise on page xx. Now that you are feeling calm, visualize your bed as a magic carpet and feel yourself floating in mid air. The carpet can hover or move at whatever speed you desire and go wherever you want. Now start the journey of your choice. You might want to gaze at a favourite piece of countryside from above, float over a sun-drenched beach or even travel the world. Of course, the carpet also functions in outer space, so a journey to the stars is no problem. You will find that you soon fall into a peaceful, happy sleep (and the carpet switches to autopilot as soon as you do so).

BASIC MEDITATION

I t is unfortunate that in Western society, meditation is known only for its connection with Eastern mystical religious practice. But it is far more accessible than that. And is the perfect recourse for a troubled mind when more routine relaxation exercises are not enough.

The popular view of meditation is polarized between those who believe it is an almost magical technique for attaining enlightenment, and those who think it is a load of nonsense. Neither view is especially helpful. In fact, meditation is not a single phenomenon, but a large number of techniques, that are used for a wide variety of purposes. There is nothing remotely magical about any of them. They all make use of the mind's enormous power to help us in various ways.

A SIMPLE MEDITATION

Here are instructions for a simple meditation technique that anybody can use. It is completely safe and easy to do, and has great benefits.

- You need a room where you can be quiet and won't get distracted.
- Choose a time when you are unlikely to have callers and, if possible, turn off your phone.
- The room you choose should be light, airy and neither too warm nor too cool.
- Sit comfortably on an uptight chair, with a cushion if necessary. Don't lean against the back of the chair. Sit up straight, but not so straight that you feel strained.
- Tuck in your chin slightly, close your eyes and fold your hands in your lap.
- Now start to focus on your breathing. Breathe normally through your nose. Keep your mouth lightly shut.
- Try to keep your mind on your breathing by counting your breaths. Count on each out-breath. When you get to five, go back to the beginning again.
- To begin with, you will be surprised how hard it is to do this without being distracted. You'll find yourself constantly bothered by itches, noises

coming from outdoors and wandering thoughts. Every time you feel distracted, just gently guide your thoughts back to your breathing.

- Eventually, you will find that you enter a state of deep relaxation.

USEFUL MEDITATION TIPS

- It is entirely natural to sleep when you feel relaxed, and therefore you have to learn to stay awake. If you keep your upright posture, this will help you to stay alert. (If you do fall asleep, try to carry on with your meditation when you wake up. You may find that a brief nap refreshes you.) If you really can't get over your sleepiness, give up and try another time when you are more rested.

- Once you have mastered the art of entering a meditative state without sleeping, you can make it part of your creative process and use it to assist in creative projects that you are undertaking.

- While meditating, begin to examine the creative project in question. It is important that you don't start to analyse it or worry about problems you are having. That is now what meditation is all about. Try to keep the project in mind and simply examine it as though you were a stranger seeing it for the first time. Don't evaluation or criticize, just LOOK.

- While in a state of deep meditation, you are in close proximity to the unconscious mind but, because you are fully conscious, when you bring your meditation to an end you will remember any thoughts that occurred to you.

- This is the point at which you will start to have useful insights into your project. Aspects of your work that have so far eluded you will suddenly become apparent. You may well find that answers to problems that have been bothering you will now pop into your mind.

- Meditate regularly. As a beginner, it is only necessary to do ten minutes (which will seem like an eternity). As you progress, the meditation can be extended to twenty or thirty minutes.

- The benefits of meditation are manifold. You will find that you feel more relaxed, more able to think creatively and that your general health will improve.

ADVANCED MEDITATION

Once you have mastered a basic level of meditation there are several other more advanced methods you can try. Here are just two, to get you started.

FOLLOWING THE BREATH

AIM This is an extremely powerful form of meditation that has its origins in Zen, though here it is devoid of any religious connotations and can be practised by those of any persuasion.

TASK Start with the Basic Meditation exercise on page xx. After you have completed the breath-counting exercise five times, stop counting and simply follow your breathing. This might seem less demanding than keeping count of your breaths but the opposite is true. To keep focused on your breath without the help of counting is really difficult. The tendency is for your mind to wander but you must keep bringing it back to your breathing. Next, try to find your hara. This is a spot, a couple of centimetres below the navel that, if stimulated properly, will release a great flood of energy to power your meditation. Just try to feel that spot and, as you breathe in, direct the air to the hara. Create a gentle (repeat gentle) pressure in your lower abdomen. Once you have got this working properly all you need to do is follow your breathing without letting your attention waver. This may at first appear a very plain and boring exercise but do not be fooled, it is immensely powerful and, if cultivated properly, will bring great benefits in health, freedom from stress and mental development. Just as sitting in the cockpit of an aircraft can give you no idea of what it's like to fly one, so the early stages of meditation do not give you an inkling of all that you will be able to learn later.

CHAKRA MEDITATION

AIM This is an Indian meditation system that relies on seven chakras or
energy centres that correspond roughly to the main endocrine glands.
The aim is to stimulate each centre and release its energy.

TASK Before attempting this you need to work on Basic Meditation on page
13. To start chakra meditation you begin as usual with counting your
breaths. After five repetitions you can stop counting and begin to
concentrate on the lowest of the chakras (see diagram). A warm glow
should spread through the affected region. Once you get proficient at this,
move to the next chakra and so on until you reach the final one on the
crown of the head. Each chakra is associated with a particular aspect of the
personality. These are:

1. **ROOT:** Base of spine – Survival, grounding
2. **SACRAL:** Abdomen, genitals, lower back – Sexuality, emotions, desire
3. **SOLAR PLEXUS:** Solar plexus – Power, will
4. **HEART:** Central chest – Love, relationships
5. **THROAT:** Throat – Communication
6. **BROW:** Brow – Intuition, imagination
7. **CROWN:** Top of head - Awareness

HELP
This is a technique that will take a lifetime to perfect, so don't
expect rapid results. Try to practise every day and you will find that,
little by little, your ability increases.

SELF-HYPNOSIS

Self-hypnosis is a simple, but very effective technique that allows you to liberate your mind from the bonds that normally constrain it.

Hypnosis uses a state of deep relaxation to allow suggestions to be fed directly into the unconscious mind, without going through the unusual process of comprehension and evaluation that the conscious mind applies to new information. It is possible to buy hypnotic tapes that promise to boost your creativity, but the problem with these is that they rely on allowing a disembodied voice to lull you into a hypnotic state and then whisper suggestions to you. Some people find it scary to allow a complete stranger such a degree of access to their mind. The alternative therefore is to do the job yourself. This is quite a simple technique that anyone can learn.

First, choose a time when you will be alone and undisturbed. You should practise your self-hypnosis at a regular time and not just whenever the fancy takes you. Make sure, as far as possible, that you are not going to be interrupted (for example, turn off your phone).

Thoughts
The average number of thoughts that humans
are believed to experience each day is a whopping 70,000.

PHASE 1 – RELAXATION

- Sit or lie in a comfortable position. It is possible that you will fall asleep at some point, so make sure that the position you have chosen will allow you to do this safely.
- Close your eyes and start to breathe slowly and deeply. Focus all your attention on your breathing. Keep this up until you feel completely comfortable.
- Now, start relaxing all the muscles in your body. Begin with your feet. First, clench all the muscles tightly. Hold for a few seconds and then relax. Repeat the process. You will find that the process of tensing and then relaxing your muscles leaves them feeling completely relaxed.
- Move up to your calves and once again tense the muscles for a few seconds and then relax. Repeat this process.
- Slowly work your way up the body, tensing and relaxing each group of muscles as you go. The groups to work on are: feet, calves, thighs, buttocks, stomach, back, arms, hands, chest, neck, face and scalp. Make especially sure that you relax the muscles in your stomach, chest and face, as these are areas that are particularly prone to tension.
- Now your whole body should be completely relaxed. You are ready to enter the hypnotic state.

The technique outlined above will, if used regularly, give your creative powers a boost. Once you are adept at inducing the hypnotic state, you can use it to tackle specific problems. For example, if you have reached a point in one of your projects where you don't know how to progress to the next phase, the tape can be adapted specifically to encourage you to find an answer to your problem. This is a very useful way of getting to grips with a creative block.

PHASE 2 – INDUCING HYPNOSIS

In preparation for this phase, you should record a tape to listen to, containing instructions for deepening the hypnotic state. Talk in a quiet, calm voice and repeat each instruction several times. There are several things you need to include on the tape, as follows:

- Tell yourself to imagine that you are in a warm, safe, comfortable place. This can be anywhere you like. You can use a real place, or an imaginary one if that suits you better. The only requirement is that the place should give you a feeling of complete security.
- Now you are ready to deepen your hypnotic state. Do this by counting down slowly from a hundred. You will quite probably go to sleep during this phase (though it doesn't matter if you don't). Just keep listening to your own voice as it soothes and relaxes you.
- Now you are ready for the suggestions. These can be of any sort you like but, for present purposes, we will look at suggestions that will improve your creativity. It is very important that all the suggestions you use are positive and encouraging. Don't tell yourself not to do things. Concentrate on telling yourself that you are a creative and original person who has a constant supply of bright ideas. (If you want, visualize yourself fishing for bright ideas in an ocean. The ideas look like brightly coloured fish, and you have a net full of the ones you have already caught. Alternatively, you could visualize the creative urge flowing through you like a warm liquid that enters and soothes every part of your body.)

Symbolism
As those who invest in dream dictionaries can attest, dreams almost never represent what they actually are. The unconscious mind strives to make connections with concepts you will understand, so dreams are largely symbolic representations.

- Before you finish, you might choose to include a number of affirmations that will help boost the positive view of your creative abilities that you are trying to create. Here are some examples:

I am a channel for creativity.

I have well-developed creative talents.

My work is productive and fulfilling.

I feel the creative urge within me all the time.
I am always open to the flow of new ideas.

I am confident and competent in my creative work.

I am eager to experience my creative energy.

My life is rewarding and creative.

I am willing to think creatively.

- Finally, bring yourself gently out of the hypnotic state. Do this by counting backwards from ten to one. Pause during the count to tell yourself that you are waking up. When you get to the end of the count, tell yourself to wake up and open your eyes. It is important that waking up from the hypnotized state is done gently.
- Always have a pad and pen beside you so that you can jot down any good ideas that occurred to you while in the hypnotic state. Remember that such ideas are highly volatile and will evaporate within seconds of your waking, so it is important to catch them straight away.

THE LAND OF NOD

Sleep is hugely important to us, although we are still not sure what its real purpose is. We do know that if we do not get enough sleep, we suffer.

At first we are simply tired, grumpy and anxious, but if the sleep deprivation continues, we will start to develop symptoms of severe mental disturbance. In extreme cases, where people are deprived of sleep over a long period, they may die.

As we have already seen, the unconscious mind is where creativity takes place. The only time we are aware of visiting this area of the mind is during our dreams. We all dream, every night. Some people are very aware of their dreams and remember them in detail; others say that they never dream, but this is not so. They simple don't recall their dreams when they wake up. The first dream of the night is the shortest, and may last no more than ten minutes or so. After eight hours of sleep, dreams can last from forty-five minutes to an hour.

Dreams occur during Rapid Eye Movement (REM) sleep. If you watch someone who is having a dream, you can actually see the eyes moving under the eyelids. During an REM period, it is common to have more than one dream. The dreams are separated by short arousals that are usually forgotten. Sleep researchers tell us that dreams are not recalled unless the sleeper awakens directly from the dream, rather than after going on to other stages of sleep.

SLEEP AND CREATIVITY

What has all this to do with creativity? Dreams may be about our fears and anxieties, but sometimes they contain the answers to problems that have been bothering us. In some instances, these will be creative problems to which we have so far failed to find an answer. If we are alert to what the unconscious tells us, we may well find the solutions we seek. Dream messages nearly always arrive in a disguised form, however, so the meaning may not be immediately apparent. This is why it is necessary to take careful note of dreams in order to work out what messages they contain.

SLEEP ON IT

Did your mother ever encourage you to solve a problem by saying, 'Sleep on it, things always look better in the morning'? She had a point. While you sleep, your mind keeps on working and, humiliating though it is to admit, the mind often gets on much better without our (rational) interruptions. Try the following experiment.

- Take a work problem to bed with you and go through the points carefully before you go to sleep. Don't just glance at a few papers, but really make an effort to wrestle with the problem and solve it by using your normal powers of reasoning. If you're really tired and find yourself thinking rubbish, so much the better! This is just the sort of state of mind you need to be in.
- When you feel that you really can't go on any longer, it's time to turn in for the night.
- If it's practicable, put your notebook (or some notes on a sheet of paper) under your pillow. This will ensure that the problem you're wrestling with will be high on the agenda when your subconscious kicks in after you fall asleep.

As soon as you wake, you're likely to find that you have several solutions to the problem. Write them down immediately!

Yawns

It is thought that a yawn works to send more oxygen to the brain, therefore working to cool it down and wake it up.

LUCID DREAMS

Maddeningly, creativity does not reside in the conscious part of the mind, where we can access it readily, but in the unconscious part, over which we have little, if any, control. One way to access this creativity is through lucid dreams.

Beneath the thin crust of rationality lies a great ocean of ideas that, if we're lucky, will sometimes pop into consciousness to illuminate our rather dreary thought processes. So do you just have to sit around waiting for inspiration? Certainly not! In fact that is the very worst thing you can do. Inspiration is rather like lightning – in that although you certainly can't control it, you can encourage it to strike. Remember Benjamin Franklin? When he wanted to study lightning, he famously flew a kit bearing a large metal key into a thunderstorm – dangerous but effective! You needn't do anything that risky. In fact, this technique for awaking the unconscious is decidedly restful.

BEAUTIFUL DREAMER

There is a technique known as lucid dreaming in which (although you are asleep and dreaming) you know that you are dreaming and you are able to take charge of the dream and steer it in whatever direction you want it to go. The advantages of this are enormous. In a dream there are no limits to what you can do: you can fly, walk through walls, speak any language you wish or even visit other worlds. The opportunities for creative thinking are almost limitless for someone who possesses such abilities.

Instructions for lucid dreaming
- The first essential is to spend time increasing your dream awareness. At the very least, when you wake up, spend the first few minutes recalling your dreams and jotting down notes.
- The next step is to learn to look for what are called 'dream signs'. The problem with dreams is that while we are involved in them, they often seem completely normal. The fact that the sky is green and you are wearing a tuxedo and speaking Russian will not faze you one bit. These

departures from normality are called dream signs and you have to train yourself to look for them.

- Next, you have to train yourself to use a sign that will tell you that you are dreaming. This can be absolutely anything you please, though it needs to be something you would not normally do. For example, you might decide that once you suspect yourself of dreaming, you could tug your left earlobe with your right hand.

- Finally, you need to learn how to prolong a lucid dream. The problem is that many people, as soon as they realize they are dreaming, tend to wake up. This is definitely not the aim. Lucid dreamers use a technique called 'dream spinning' to combat this: the moment they realize that they are dreaming, they make their dream body spin like a ballet dancer. This may sound a trifle eccentric, but experienced lucid dreamers insist that it is the best way to prolong a dream.

FLOPPY WATCHES

AIM This exercise is named in honour of Salvador Dalí, who is said to have invented it. As with most creativity exercises it provides a way of bypassing the conscious mind and getting at the unconscious, the source of most creativity.

TASK Just on the edge of sleep the mind finds itself in an area where the subconscious is very close and can be briefly glimpsed. The trouble is that you then fall asleep and probably forget everything you saw in this zone of twilight. The Spanish surrealist Salvador Dalí used to overcome this by using a technique in which he would let himself doze in an armchair. In one hand he would hold a metal spoon and on the floor he placed a metal dish. Just as he was about to fall asleep he'd drop the spoon and the resulting crash would wake him up. He then remembered vividly the strange visions he had just experienced. If you wonder whether it worked you only have to take a quick glance at his paintings. Now you try it.

UNCONSCIOUS
INCUBATION

While Leonardo da Vinci was painting *The Last Supper* in the refectory of the Convent of Santa Maria delle Grazie, he frequently worked from dawn to dusk.

But from time to time, he would take a break and apparently spend time doing nothing. The prior, who was responsible for the work, was annoyed and repeatedly asked him to get on with the job and finish it. Leonardo was unmoved and so, eventually, the prior complained to the duke. When Leonardo was asked why he took so much time off from his work he replied, 'The greatest geniuses sometimes accomplish more when they work less.'

Clearly, Leonardo knew the value of 'unconscious incubation' – the process in which the unconscious mind keeps working on a problem while the conscious mind stops thinking about it. It is a humbling thought that the mind frequently works better without our interference. You have probably had the experience of wrestling with a problem without coming to a solution and then, after you have stopped thinking about it, the answer suddenly comes to you in a flash of inspiration. The unconscious mind is a great mystery. If it were merely a storehouse for all the things that we don't need to think about immediately, that would be quite understandable. But the unconscious is far more complex than that. It keeps thinking all the time, whether we are awake or asleep. From time to time, it throws up notions in a way that seems quite random. Certainly, it is outside our conscious control. The activities of the unconscious are many and varied. It can, for example, blind us to thoughts that we would rather not entertain. Alternatively, it can force such thoughts upon us and make us incapable of thinking about anything else. Sometimes it generates thoughts that seem to have no immediate relevance to anything. Are such thoughts truly random, or does the unconscious have some purpose of its own that the conscious mind can't penetrate?

WORKING ON A PROBLEM

This is not the place to go too deeply into the workings of the mind. Let us confine ourselves to ways in which 'unconscious incubation' can be used to help our creative powers. Although there is no sure way of making the unconscious work on a problem, there are things we can do to give it encouragement. Here are some of them:

- Spend as much time as you can attempting to work out the problem with your conscious mind. Use all your ingenuity to try to find a solution. It doesn't matter if all the ideas you come up with are no good. The important thing is to focus your mind upon the problem and to consider it from every angle.
- Write down all the possible solutions or, at the very least, make notes of the difficulties you encounter and the reasons that no solution has been found. It is very important to go through this phase of the operation as thoroughly as possible. The unconscious mind will not provide flashes of inspiration unless you have exhausted more conventional methods first.
- Now, take a break. It really doesn't matter what you do but it should be something that has no relation to your problem.
- Leave your problem alone for at least twenty-four hours. If no solution presents itself, go back to thinking consciously about possible solutions.
- With luck, one of two things will eventually happen. The unconscious may throw up a fully formed solution. Or, while you are working on the problem with your conscious mind, you will suddenly be able to work out what to do, whereas before you drew a blank.
- Because the unconscious is utterly unpredictable, there is no guarantee that a solution will be forthcoming at all. However, it sometimes happens that the problem will incubate for months or even years. This is why it is important always to keep a note of all your ideas. You just never know what is going to come to the surface.

HELP
Don't forget to write your ideas down as soon as possible.
Inspiration achieved by this method will evaporate like morning
mist if not recorded instantly.

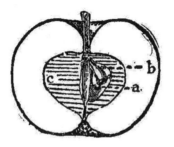

THE ADVENTURES OF HUCKLEBERRY FINN
In the late summer of 1883, at Quarry Farm, in southern New York State, Mark Twain finally finished a book that, according to his own account, he had 'been fooling over for seven years'. This is a clear example of the way in which creative tasks cannot be hurried. Doubtless if Twain had tried to force the pace and finish his work quickly, it would have been a much lesser book than the one we now know – *The Adventures of Huckleberry Finn*. It took seven years of unconscious incubation before it was finally fully formed and ready to be published.

CONCENTRATON

Many people think that creative work is all about chilling out and having wonderful ideas while in a state of mental calm. This is certainly one face of creativity, but it is not the only one.

Once you have the ideas, it takes hard work to translate them into reality, and hard work takes concentration. Concentration is the powerhouse of memory. No matter how many tips and tricks you learn from this book, your memory will not reach its full potential unless you learn how to concentrate. This is not something that comes easily to most of us nor, in spite of its huge importance, is it something that we are taught at home or at school. When I was at school, the teachers would yell, 'Concentrate, boy!' but they might just as well have said, 'Levitate!' for all the good it did. I didn't know how to concentrate – not at will, anyway. Like most people, I could concentrate furiously on what interested me – a good book would do the trick – but had trouble bending my mind to Latin case endings or quadratic equations.

CONCENTRATION TECHNIQUE

Concentration is considered a necessary skill in many Far Eastern cultures, and there are techniques for teaching it. Here is one of them, which you might find useful. It is several millennia old, but none the worse for that:

- Light a candle and set it on a table in front of you.
- Stare at the candle for a couple of minutes. Try to remember every detail – the colour and texture of the wax, the appearance of the flame and the way it moves. Fix it all in your mind.
- Now close your eyes and try to retain the image of the candle in your mind's eye for as long as you can.
- Your first efforts will probably be pitiful. This exercise looks easy but isn't.
- Keep trying again and again. Eventually, you will be able to hold the image of the candle in your mind's eye for as long as you wish.

CONCENTRATION TRAINING

What other things must you do when you concentrate? One is to structure your time. Set aside a specific time for doing a particular task and try not to deviate from that. It is quite natural to sit down to a task, especially one that you don't really enjoy, and then think of something important you need to attend to. Then you fancy a coffee. Then you go to see if the post has arrived. Then the phone rings and you spend time chatting. Then, since you're already on the phone, you call a friend and waste some more time chatting. If you recognize this scenario, you not only need to practise concentration regularly, but also to structure, your time. Make yourself a timetable and slot in all the tasks you hope to accomplish.

When you construct the timetable, bear in mind the way your day normally unfolds. Don't allot complicated tasks to times when you are usually disturbed. Remember that there are quiet times that often don't get used (early mornings, for example), which are really valuable if you need to work undisturbed.

If, as your work progresses, you find that your initial time estimates were faulty, you can correct them. That doesn't matter. But what does matter is that you stick to your task until it is accomplished and do NOT let yourself be distracted.

Incidentally, if you think I'm one of life's naturally ordered workers, who concentrates effortlessly, you'd be quite wrong. Everything I've written above is the product of bitter experience and oceans of wasted time. But now this section of the book is finished and I'm going for a coffee (after amending my timetable to show that it took me twenty minutes less than I'd planned).

Take a couple of minutes to consider whatever task is before you. Don't just rush into it, but consciously decide what methods you could use to complete it, and how long it should take. Once you have decided on the length of the session, stick to that decision and let nothing stop you.

PICKING PAIRS

AIM This is a way to build your concentration. It looks really simple but unless you remain completely focused you will not do very well.

TASK Take a look at the rows of figures below. In each row you must pick out pairs of adjacent numbers that add up to 10. For example, in this line: 3 4 6 5 2 8 9 3 7, there are three pairs (4 + 6, 2 + 8 and 3 + 7). If you had a line containing 4 6 4 that would count as TWO pairs.

1 4 7 3 7 3 5 4 6 2 8 5 4 7 5 5 8 1 9 7

3 6 4 4 5 7 3 7 2 8 2 3 7 6 2 8 6 9 1 8

5 3 7 5 2 4 6 7 2 2 8 7 3 8 2 8 7 3 7 2

8 4 6 4 3 7 5 5 7 3 6 2 8 5 8 9 1 6 4 6

9 0 4 6 3 5 5 1 9 4 5 2 8 2 3 1 9 0 2 8

Unconsciousness
If your brain loses blood for 8 to 10 seconds,
you will lose consciousness.

NOSE TO THE GRINDSTONE

AIM This is an exercise in applied concentration. Previous tasks will have shown you how to boost your powers of concentration but now it's time to take your newfound skills and put them to the test in a real world situation.

TASK Choose a job that will keep you occupied for about 30 minutes. It needn't be a specific type of task. It could be anything from writing a letter to mending the car. The main requirement is that it should be something requiring your undivided attention. Now structure your time. Divide the task into parts (such as planning, gathering materials and so on) and decide approximately how long each part will take you. You can readjust your assessment as you go along if necessary. Add an inducement to keep yourself happy. Promise yourself a coffee break or a snack when you've finished. Now the hard part: once you've started DO NOT ALLOW YOURSELF TO BE DISTRACTED. Choose a time when you are unlikely to be interrupted by visitors or phone calls. Work steadily and resist the temptation to break off and daydream. If you encounter problems do not give up and do something else, but think your way through them until you have a solution.

DOING THE TASK

If you had real problems, try again but start with a much shorter task. Judge from your first experience and decide just how long you think you can work for without getting distracted. Once you have found a length of time that suits you, keep practising and you will eventually be able to concentrate for longer periods.

HELP

Try to work in an atmosphere that suits you. Some people need peace and quiet in order to concentrate, others prefer to have music or chatter going on in the background. Some can work quite happily on their own, while some need to be with other people. Look for situations in which you find it easy to concentrate and use them to handle other tasks.

CREATIVITY

Everybody has the capacity to be creative. The creative urge is something that is uniquely human. Why then do some people produce a constant flow of new ideas and others don't?

Part of the answer is to do with natural ability. Just as some people are good at running, playing chess, swimming or learning languages, others are good at having ideas. But confidence and self-esteem also play a large part in the process.

If you believe that you are creative and that your ideas are valuable, you will be motivated to produce more of them. If, on the other hand, you have never been encouraged to consider yourself capable of producing bright ideas, the likelihood is that you will not produce many an, if you do have an idea, you will automatically assume that it is of no real value. Fear of ridicule and lack of self-esteem are major disabilities in the creative process.

GETTING STARTED

If you follow the exercises in this book you will find that you have a creative spark that can be fanned into a flame. Creativity cannot be taught in the way that you can teach, say, maths or science, but it can be encouraged to grow. If you make your mind a fertile ground for good ideas, you will find that they flourish there. You do not need to be a genius, you don't even have to be especially clever, but you do need to open yourself up to the creative spirit that lies within your unconscious mind. Once you start to have ideas, you will generate more; and once your ideas start to be appreciated by other people, you will find yourself motivated to continue developing your creative powers.

Most importantly of all, make a conscious decision that from now on you ARE a creative person.

• In future, all your ideas (however trivial they may seem) have to be collected and kept. You never know when an idea will come in handy, or when something that seemed unimportant when you first thought of it will suddenly become of vital importance.

- Pick some creative projects to get yourself started. It helps to have several projects on the go at the same time, as they tend to cross-fertilize each other. It also helps if the projects are of quite different types.
- Work on your projects regularly and methodically. Don't ever just sit around waiting for inspiration. If one project gets bogged down, turn to another and work on that. Make sure that you set yourself goals and deadlines – if you don't do this, you may find that you run out of steam and fail to finish things you've started.
- Try to keep your attitude as flexible as possible. Your unconscious mind has an agenda of its own and, in order for your efforts to succeed, you need to be prepared to change your plans to accommodate whatever your unconscious prompts you to do.
- Remember to have fun! Creativity is hard work but it is also enjoyable. Don't get so focused on attaining your goal that you forget to enjoy the creative process.
- Remember that having bright ideas, though very important, is only a part of the creative process. Once you have the idea you then have to work hard to bring it to fruition. This is the part of the process that defeats many would-be creative people. They enjoy the processes by which bright ideas are born but lack the energy to see their project through to the end. What a waste of good ideas! Make sure that you are a worker as well as a dreamer.

CHARACTERISTICS OF CREATIVE PEOPLE

Creative people have a number of things in common. Not all of them will exhibit every one of the characteristics below but, generally, creative people tend to conform to these descriptions.

1. ENERGY
Creative individuals tend to be energetic. Though they may have bouts of laziness (like most of us), they do manage to overcome this and get things done. They have a deeply felt need to be productive, because they get a strong emotional boost from creative work.

2. CURIOSITY
Creative individuals are very curious. They tend to question everything and try to see the world from new perspectives. Their questioning way sometimes irritate others who are of a more practical turn of mind.

3. IDEAS FOR THEIR OWN SAKE
They love ideas for their own sake. Even if an idea is of no apparent practical value, they will investigate it if it seems interesting enough. However, they can be fickle and will drop an idea in which their interest has waned, even if it means abandoning a project.

4. PUTTING IDEAS INTO PRACTICE
They often enjoy making things. This can manifest itself in all sorts of ways, but they always get a great deal of satisfaction from seeing an idea turned into a finished product. Again, they can be fickle and suddenly get bored with a project before it is brought to a conclusion.

5. PLAYFULNESS
They are often playful and quite happy to mess about with activities that others might regard as childish. They are not especially bothered about appearing serious or adult.

6. IMAGINATION AND FANTASY

Creative individuals are very adept at using imagination and fantasy; they also have a strong desire to use the things they dream up as a basis for projects. They are far more concerned about using an interesting idea than producing a practical outcome.

7. FOCUSING ON PROJECTS

As long as the ideas they are using remain sufficiently arresting, creative people are able to remain focused on a project for as long as it takes to bring it to a successful conclusion. They can be quite obsessive and frequently become deeply involved in a project.

8. DEALING WITH SETBACKS

They are very resilient and not easily put off by setbacks. For them, the most important thing is to continue to create at all costs.

9. INTUITION

Creative people are closely in touch with the promptings of their unconscious. They are very intuitive and tend to feel their way to solutions rather than work them out logically. However, they may well need others to help with the nitty-gritty of their projects, as they are prone to overlook practicalities and irritating details.

10. CHURNING OUT IDEAS

Creative people are more interested in having ideas than in exploiting them. They are often quite happy to leave the development phase to others.

10%
The old adage of humans only using 10% of their brain is not true.
Every part of the brain has a known function.

WINE WOBBLE

For this task, take a wine glass, fill it with water and place it in a position where it cannot be picked up without causing all the water to be spilt. This last condition is very important. Most people who pick up a full glass will spill just a little liquid; the challenge in this case is to find a method that guarantees all the water is spilt.

RANDOM STANZAS

AIM This is another exercise that will allow you to get past that creative block and reach the fertile soil of your unconscious mind.

TASK Take some small slips of paper and write one of your favourite words on one side of each one. Favourite words? That's right, just choose words that you really like the sound of. You need at least 100 words but the more the better. When you've got all your words ready, turn the slips of paper face down on the table and give them a good stir so that you have no idea which is which. Then start to pick words at random. Pick as many as you like and then, when you decide you have enough, start to move them around to form sentences. Of course, you won't get complete grammatical sentences without much use of your imagination, but you will get phrases that suggest ideas to you. How you use these phrases is up to you. You could write a poem, produce the first line of a story to find a key phrase that will help you solve a problem.

Wattage
While awake, your brain generates between 10 and 23 watts
of power – or enough energy to power a light bulb.

THINK CREATIVE

AIM The only way to be creative is to believe that you are creative. This task gives you a push in the right direction.

TASK If you want to increase your creativity you have to work at it day and night. Your first task is simply to convince yourself that you are a creative person. From now on your thoughts, experiences, dreams, doodles and even the things you overhear other people say, will all be grist to your mill. Collect everything. Throw nothing away. All of it, sooner or later, will prove useful. Here are just a few of the things you can do to enhance your creativity:

- Keep a diary or, at the very least, a notebook of your ideas.
- Pay close attention to dreams. They are often a good source of inspiration.
- If you doodle during idle moments, hang on to your doodles.
- Make a point of having new experiences that give you a chance to broaden your mind.
- Listen not just to what people say, but the way that they say it. Casual remarks made by other people can be an excellent trigger for bright ideas.
- Never question whether you have a creative gift (plenty of other people will do that for you). Just keep on creating and, eventually, someone will spot your potential.
- Always pay attention to other people's best ideas, not to copy them but because one good idea can often spark off another.

Stimulation
A stimulating environment for a child can make the difference between a 25% greater ability to learn or 25% less in an environment with little stimulation.

TWENTY QUESTIONS

AIM This used to be a very popular game but, with the rise of mass communication and electronic entertainment, most people have either never played it or have forgotten how.

TASK One person thinks of an object, person, animal, book or whatever. The others (as many or as few as you like) are allowed to ask 20 questions and must then try to work out what their opponent is thinking of. This is a very useful game to play with kids (try it on a long journey). It is also good for adults who can, if they wish, play it at a more advanced level. The thing you think of can be as simple as 'cat' or as complicated as Heisenberg's Uncertainty Principle.

TO BOLDLY GO...

AIM Creativity is about going beyond the obvious until you get to some new place you've never visited before. This exercise will help you do that.

TASK Take any common household object, a paperclip for example, and try to come up with 50 (yes, 50) new uses for it. Why so many? Because after a couple of dozen or so you'll be struggling and then you'll really have to dig deep to come up with the rest. When you arrive at the stage when you feel you have nothing left to give, take a rest from racking your brains and do something different.

HELP
Don't try to complete this exercise all at once. The trick is to push yourself to your limit, and then do something else while you wait for your subconscious to mull the task over. You can work at this over days or even weeks if you want to. If you persist you'll be amazed how many new ideas you can find.

ORIGINAL THOUGHT

From an early age, we are taught to think in a certain way: to be rational, to do what has been done before and not to defy convention.

Subliminally, we're also taught to follow the crowd, not to take chances and to trust neither our instincts nor our imagination (which, after all, only produces 'flights of fancy' that get us nowhere). It consequently becomes an ingrained habit to look for solutions to problems by referring to what has been done before.

This way of thinking is a 'box' that hinders our ability to think creatively. We end up doing what military leaders tend to do (as observed by military historians) – they develop tactics that would have brought a speedy triumph in the most recently fought war but that prove to be useless when applied to the next war that comes along. Also, the brain itself is wired to think in certain ways – this, too, is a 'box'. To think creatively, we need to get out of both boxes. Do these exercises to start the journey and find out how boxy your brain is!

ORIGINAL THINKER

This test will surprise you. It shows very clearly how our brains are wired in certain ways. When you have done it yourself, try it out on family and friends to see if their response is the same.

Complete the following calculations:

$$1 + 5 = \qquad 7 - 1 =$$
$$4 + 2 = \qquad 8 - 2 =$$
$$3 + 3 = \qquad 0 + 6 =$$

- Now repeat the word 'six' out loud for about fifteen seconds.
- NAME A VEGETABLE.
- Now look at the answer box on the bottom of page 94.

TESTING YOUR ORIGINALITY
OF THOUGHT

This game demonstrates your ability to think outside the box, but only if you give yourself time. Have a good, long look at the eight small images below. What could they be? There is no single correct answer. In fact, the more answers you can come up with, the better. Take your time, because the longer you take, the more likely you are to get new and better ideas.

Once you've had a good look at all eight images, use the scoring system explained on page 92 to see how well you've done.

There is no time limit on this task.

So how did you do?

- The first time you attempt this task give yourself one point for each idea you come up with. At the end of the task add up your total number of points and see how well you did.

10–15 = poor
16–40 = average
41–60 = good
above 60 = excellent

- Return to the task a little later (next day, for example) and try again. This time, give yourself three points for each new idea. Again, tot up your final score and measure your originality of thought using the following scoring system.

9–12 = poor
15–24 = average
27–36 = good
above 36 = excellent

- Finally, come back to the test a week later and have one last go. This is the most exciting part of the test. By now, you should be right out of ideas; everything that 'makes sense' will have occurred to you long ago. On the other hand, your mind will have been turning over the problem subconsciously. This time, give yourself five points per idea.

0–15 = poor
20–30 = average
35–50 = good
over 50 = excellent

As you will have noticed, once you had exhausted all the 'rational' options and were forced to use your imagination (and had started to think outside the box in a more creative way), many more possibilities will have sprung to mind!

FREE THINKER

AIM This exercise will loosen the grip of your conscious mind and allow those nuggets of creative gold from the unconscious to shine through.

TASK this is a version of the free association technique used by psychiatrists to help patients discover their unconscious motives. Here we are not concerned with disturbing thoughts but with creative ideas. First, make yourself comfortable. If you own a tape recorder, switch it on. Now pick a word at random and see what other word it suggests to you, then let the new word suggest another word and so on. For example, you might start with 'lamp'. From this you could go to 'light', 'dark', 'night', 'stars', 'travel', 'journey', 'adventure', 'distance' and so on. This technique works best if you don't think too hard about your choices. Run rapidly through a string of related words. The tape recorder will allow you to look back at your stream of consciousness.

Synapses

There are anywhere from 1,000 to 10,000 synapses for each neuron. Synapses are junctions that allow electrical pulses and chemicals to pass between two nerve cells.

HELP

This task provides two things of real value. First, the exercise will loosen you up mentally. By thinking freely you will break the bonds that restrain you from creative thought. Second, when you re-examine your recorded thoughts you will often find that the words suggest a train of thought that you can use in another context.

REMOVING
THINKING BLOCKS

One of the worst enemies of creative thinking is the dangerous habit of relying on old-style thinking to tackle a new problem. This is very seductive, because it produces a known result at a predictable cost.

Young people, who by definition haven't got much experience of anything, are inclined to think out a problem from scratch. Their elders, however, make up for their relatively slower thought processes by relying on experience. And what is experience? It's remembering the thing that worked last time. This is a disaster for creativity. It means that all the thinking within an organization ends up running on rail tracks laid by the oldest and most senior managers. The room for creative solutions is very limited or, sometimes, non-existent.

Now you may be thinking, 'How stupid to let things carry on like that. If I were in charge, I'd encourage the young people to come up with wonderful creative solutions.' The trouble is that many new ideas simply don't work. The unconscious mind is excellent at producing an endless supply of ideas but these come with no guarantee of quality. In fact, the vast majority of new ideas simply don't work. To rely on new thinking to solve a problem is therefore expensive and has an uncertain outcome. If you hit a winner, you may do very well, but what if all the bright ideas that your bright young managers come up with turn out to be duds? Then you face an expensive failure, for which senior management will eventually have to carry the can. This is why people tend to play safe and go for ideas that are tried and tested. There are many ways in which our capacity for creative thinking is reduced or even eliminated. Let's look at some of them...

ORIGINAL THINKER ANSWER FROM PAGE 92
Did you say 'carrot'? When tested, 98% of people give the same answer.
This isn't magic (though at first you might think it is); instead it is a perfect
example of how, quite unwittingly, we tend to think in boxes. The moral of this
tale is: beware the box – especially the one you don't know you are in.

THE MONKEY TRAP

This famous story is often used to illustrate a problem with creative thinking. The monkey trap is a simple device that depends, for its effectiveness, on the limited thinking powers of the monkey. A hollowed-out coconut is hung from a tree. A small hole is made in the bottom of the coconut and a tempting snack is placed inside. Here's the clever bit: the hole is just big enough for the monkey to slide in his open hand, but not big enough for him to withdraw his closed fist.

The monkey smells the food, puts his hand into the hole, grasps the food and then can't pull his clenched fist through the opening. When the hunters arrive, the monkey panics, and because he is not thinking clearly, he still tries to pull his closed fist through the hole. Nothing is holding him prisoner except his own defective thinking.

THINKING THE UNTHINKABLE

Here is another story about problems with thinking. Two little boys are playing table tennis, when their one and only ball falls into a small hole in the floor. It is a very snug fit and there is no room for the boys to get their fingers around the ball to pull it out. They are afraid they will get into trouble if they confess to having lost the ball, so they cannot call an adult for help. There are no tools in the room. They try blowing into the house but, although he ball rises when they blow down the side, they aren't able to catch it before it sinks back down again. Eventually, they have another idea and get the ball out of the hole.

If you ask people how this was down, they tend to fall into three groups. There are those who have no idea at all. There are those who do have an idea but are unwilling to propose it. And there are the very few who get the right answer. Why? Because the answer is that one of the kids urinated into the hole and floated the ball to the surface. Gross? Oh, yes. But that is the point. What puts people off seeing the answer is that it calls for them to think something disagreeable. Creative thinking requires us to think the unthinkable.

Here are some factors that contribute to people not thinking creatively:

Habit

Habit is a terrible thing from the point of view of creativity. Unfortunately, it is often perceived as being good, because if you always do what you did the time before, you will find solutions quickly and this will appear to save money – but it is a deeply misguided policy. We need to struggle with new ideas. This is how humans progress; it is how we grow. No amount of short-term benefit can outweigh our need to discover new ideas. The motto of the college I attended was 'Do different'. I'm not usually keen on mottoes, but this is one that I would commend to anyone who wants to think creatively.

Fear

People hate to look stupid. We will do just about anything rather than admit that we don't understand what others are talking about. We keep quiet rather than offer an idea that might be dismissed or, even worse, laughed at. As long as you are afraid of what other people might think, you are never going to be a truly creative person. Creativity is all about doing new things that others will inevitably find strange, stupid or shocking. Unless you have the courage to be a leader rather than a follower, you will never use your creative powers to the full.

Laziness

Being creative sounds like a lot of fun. It is a lot of fun, but it is also a lot of hard work. Having ideas, although difficult enough in itself, is only the start of the process. These will usually be a long, hard road to travel before your idea comes to fruition. Ideas have to be refined and difficulties overcome (and there are always difficulties because nothing ever goes entirely to plan). People tend to be lazy and dislike putting in the sort of long, sustained effort that any creative project requires. Playing around with the original idea is fun, producing sample material and selling the idea to the publisher is fun, but the long slog of actually writing the book is often no fun at all. So if you want to be creative, you need to reconcile yourself to the idea that you will have to work hard to achieve what you want.

Lack of persistence

An idea, however good, will encounter resistance when it is first proposed. In fact, the more stunning and original an idea, the more resistance it will meet. Therefore, if you want your idea to succeed, you have to be prepared to push it for all you're worth. People who give up easily will never succeed in any form of creative endeavour.

Thinking about the pay-off

The rewards of creativity sometimes, but by no means always, include money and fame. But if you make these things the main object of your activity, you are unlikely to succeed. Creativity demands your full attention, and it simply won't work as a means to some other end. If, for example, you start out to write a book, you need to make it the very best book you are capable of writing, and not the one you think will get you the most attention.

DIGGING A HOLE

Here is another reason that people fail to think creatively. Imagine that you are asked to dig a hole. After a short time of digging, you have achieved a circular hole about 1 m (3.2 ft) deep. If someone then came along and said, 'Sorry, I've changed my mind, it should be dug over there', you wouldn't be too upset.

Now, after a lot of work, the hole is 3 m (7.8 ft) deep. Would you be so keen to start again if the same thing happened? No, you wouldn't. You'd be quite annoyed.

Let's say that you carry on digging. The hole is now 25 m (82 ft) deep. You have hired people to help and you have employed a mining engineer to advise on how to shore up the hole and keep it from collapsing. By now it is your hole. You are responsible for its size and shape. You are responsible for the workers on the project and they are relying on you to keep them in a job. Do you see what is happening? You have now invested so much time, energy, thought and money in this project that you would be traumatized if it were suddenly scrapped.

Now, imagine that the hole is really a piece of scientific research, a book you have been writing, a painting you have spent months on or an invention you have been trying to get marketed. You can see why people are often unwilling to think things that will rock the boat, and why they will also resist anyone who comes along and tries to criticize the project with which they are so intimately involved.

London taxi drivers

Famous for knowing all the London streets by heart,
these taxi drivers have a larger than normal hippocampus,
especially the drivers who have been on the job longest.
The study suggests that as people memorize more and more
information, this part of their brain continues to grow.

CREATIVE TIPS

It is always easier to ask for forgiveness than to ask for permission.
If you believe in your idea, you must go ahead with it at all costs. If
you wait for permission, it might never come. If you find that you
are wrong, admit it frankly and then get on with your next project.

Take a random word – the more ridiculous the better –
and try to find a way to work it into your creative project.
This exercise may seem tough and you might not see right away
how it will help but if you persist you'll be surprised at the number
of original notions that suddenly pop into your mind.

PROBLEM SOLVING

The act of solving problems is a great way to utilise the left and right sides of your brain. We require need some structure (left side) and freedom/creativity (right side) in order to arrive at the best and most effective solution. The following 10 step process should help you reach a satisfactory solution to many problems you might face.

STEP 1 Definition

This might seem obvious but you won't be able to make any progress unless you clarify what your problem is. This stage of the process will also help you establish whether your problem is actually within your grasp. For instance, if it is: 'I need to win the lotto', there sadly nothing you or anyone can do about it.

STEP 2 Establishing scope

What are the remits of your problem? If it's office related, are you endeavouring to change the culture of the whole company about a given topic, those in your wider department or just your close colleagues?

STEP 3 Cause analysis

Why is this the problem actually a problem? What are the causes?

STEP 4 Generating solutions

Brainstorm potential solutions. Note down all your ideas, however ill-conceived they might appear. Do not evaluate the ideas at this stage as it will dampen your creative drive.

STEP 5 Criteria for a successful solution

Once you have generated a number of possible solutions, through uninhibited thought it is time to assess those solutions according to your parameters. Rank the criteria in order of importance.

STEP 6 Evaluation

Analyse your solutions. Don't fall into the trap of discarding some solutions out of hand simply because they don't feel right. If they match many of the key criteria then they could be viable. Conversely, don't choose a solution by 'gut feeling' in plain ignorance of the criteria. Gut feeling is often a factor involved when people buy a new property to live in. If your key criteria are lots of space for pets and a future family it might be a mistake to choose a small and quaint cottage even though it 'feels right'.

STEP 7 Decisions, decisions
Agree on a single solution based on all the information at hand. But retain one or two other strong contenders for the solution in case unforeseen problems hamper the implementation of your first choice.

STEP 8 Putting it into practice
Implement the solution. This may be simply a case of just doing it – buying the new car you have been debating. Or, if it is a complex problem, like an office relocation it will need an action plan and various target dates for the different stages of implementation.

STEP 9 Monitor and review progress
This is essential if it is a large problem. But even if it is a smaller one, reviewing the processes you went through will help you make decisions on other problem-solving issues in the future and will probably ensure you avoid making the same mistakes.

LATERAL THINKING

The term 'lateral thinking' was coined by Edward de Bono. He offered various definitions of it, but the most striking was this: 'You cannot dig a hole in a different place by digging the same hole deeper.'

Conventional thinking plods ever onwards in only one direction, but lateral thinking tries to get a new perspective on a problem that shows it to you in an entirely different light.

Puzzles that require you to solve a problem by lateral thinking have long been popular because they allow the solver to indulge a taste for wacky, off-the-wall thinking. Someone with a good imagination and an original turn of mind is far more likely to excel at problems of this sort than someone who tries to apply conventional logic. Try solving the problems in this section and see whether you can liberate your thought processes.

THE ABSENT AUNT

Sam's mother asked him to drive down to the airport to meet his Aunt Janice who was arriving from Sydney, Australia. Sam's mother and Janice had been separated at birth, but had recently got in touch with each other. Never having seen his aunt before, Sam worried that he might not recognize her, but his mother assured him that he wouldn't have a problem. How did she know? Sam hadn't seen a photo of Janice and she hadn't seen one of him. His mother hadn't seen her sister since infancy, so how did she expect Sam to recognize her?

Answer on page 168.

DEATH OF THE DEALER

In a speakeasy somewhere in Chicago during the 1930s, a group of Mafiosi were playing poker. Some of them had been losing quite heavily and were not happy about it. Eventually one of them eyed the dealer narrowly and snarled, 'I say you're cheating!' This was unwise, to say the least. The dealer whipped out a snub-nosed Colt .45 and shot the player stone dead. The cops were called. The lieutenant in charge was a tough cookie and no slouch with a gun but, even though he was heavily armed and backed up by a deputy, he couldn't arrest any of the men present. Why not? There was no shortage of witnesses and the dealer didn't even deny what had happened.

Answer on page 168.

LAST SUPPER

Angela had been searching for Mickey and was devastated when she found him lying dead. He had been clearly been eating a meal when he died, and an iron bar lay across his back. What had happened to him?

Answer on page 168.

ODD ANIMALS

The following animals have something in common. Can you work out what it is?

Koala bear • Prairie dog • Guinea pig
Silkworm • Firefly • Bombay duck

Answer on page 168.

SUCCESSFUL PLAYERS

Five men went to a large casino in Las Vegas. They played from 9 a.m. until 3 p.m. All were professional players. They didn't stop for any breaks, nobody left and nobody joined them. They played together all day and, by the time they finished, they all had more money than when they started. How is that possible?

Answer on page 168.

SEA STORY

A certain vessel undertook an epic journey, and then arrived at a sea with no water. Even so, it was able to enter the sea and complete its journey. When the crew had completed their business, they were able to return home without difficulty. Can you name the vessel and the sea it entered?

Answer on page 168.

POLITICAL PROBLEMS

From time to time, we all fantasize about showing politicians exactly what we think of them. One man took this desire to extremes by throwing tomatoes at his local representative. He was delighted when he achieved a direct hit, but then appalled when the politician dropped dead. Why did the man die from being hit by tomatoes?

Answer on page 168.

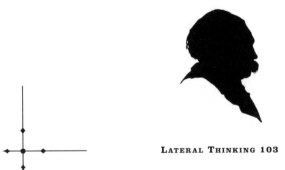

BRAINSTORMING

If you are trying to boost creativity in the workplace, the technique of brainstorming might prove valuable.

If you have never come across brainstorming before, it involves getting a group of people together with the purpose of thrashing out new ideas in a relaxed and informal atmosphere. The theory is that they should feel free to say whatever they want, no matter how silly or outrageous it might sound. The participants are encouraged to let their minds freewheel so that new and original ideas emerge. Ideally, people will be inspired by each other so that one person's crazy notion is seized on by someone else who sees how it might actually be made to work. This is the theory and, in recent years, brainstorming has become a very popular way of trying to generate new ideas. Sadly, not all brainstorms are as productive as they should be. In theory it looks easy to organize a successful brainstorming session, but in practice it is really quite difficult. To see why, you need to appreciate the characteristics of a good session.

In a corporate setting, these conditions can be hard to achieve. People who are used to a corporate atmosphere are often quite suspicious of each other and there are always undercurrents of rivalry and jealousy that make it a free exchange of ideas difficult. In many companies, there is a formal, businesslike atmosphere that discourages people from behaviour that might look silly or frivolous. Even in more laid-back companies, it would take quite a lot of courage for an employee to say something radical in front of senior colleagues. For such a session to work, it needs to be headed by a senior figure who takes the lead in creating the right atmosphere.

At its best, brainstorming is a wonderful demonstration of how chaos can be used to encourage creative thought. If you get the right group of people there will be a lively, thought-provoking discussion in which all will feel free to participate. The outcome will be a mass of ideas that can then be sorted and evaluated using the idea shuffling technique. A bad brainstorming session, however, is not just useless but actually damaging. At some sessions people compete madly to get the boss's attention and approval, pour scorn on colleagues' ideas and behave as though they were deadly rivals (which they were) rather than a team fired by enthusiasm and cooperation.

So be warned: if you brainstorm you must take great pains to get it right or you may end up doing more harm than good.

In a good brainstorm the participants should:

- Feel relaxed.
- Exhibit genuine enthusiasm.
- Be unafraid of speaking in front of colleagues and senior managers.
- Be confident enough to propose apparently crazy ideas.
- Be willing to ask silly questions.
- Be confident that any good ideas they propose will not be stolen by others.
- Be confident that any criticisms they make will not be held against them in future.
- Be confident that they will not be ridiculed by colleagues.

10 TIPS FOR ORGANIZING A PRODUCTIVE SESSION:

1. Groups should be kept small

If you have more than a dozen participants, the atmosphere will not be intimate enough.

2. Seating is important

Seat people around a table so that they can interact easily. If you use a more formal seating arrangement, people will feel inhibited.

3. Make the aims clear

You must make sure that people understand the purpose of the session. At the start, outline what you hope to achieve.

4. Don't evaluate

At this stage, all ideas are good. If someone says something wacky, that's fine. Just note everything and keep it for later.

5. Make sure that participants listen to each other

Show all participants respect and make sure that others follow your lead. Encourage people to enlarge on the ideas offered by other participants. Be very clear that no one is to ridicule suggestions made by other participants.

6. Use the china egg technique

Farmers sometimes use a china egg to encourage hens to lay. You must do a similar thing. Lead the way by offering some wild, unconventional ideas. If people see you do it, they will feel free to follow your example.

7. Try to generate as many ideas as possible

At this stage, quantity is important. The quality of the ideas can be assessed later.

8. Keep the atmosphere informal and relaxed

Meet somewhere away from the usual working environment, preferably not a conference centre (because they all look like extensions of the office). Consider providing a meal – eating will relax the participants and they'll feel the need to repay your generosity by coming up with ideas.

9. Keep them interested

While making sure that participants don't stray from the task in hand, try to keep them relaxed and interested. Have breaks during which people can chat informally.

10. Keep a record

Record the session, preferably using a tape recorder, rather than having someone take notes. Having your words written down is a bit intimidating, but people soon forget about a tape recorder.

BRAINSTORMING

AIM This is a creativity task for at least two people (preferably more). It can be used for anything from solving problems to outlining a film, play or other artistic endeavour.

TASK It is important that a brainstorming session should not be allowed to become a simple committee meeting. We all know how much committees achieve. The idea is that a group of people toss around ideas completely off the top of their head and then try to use them to resolve a particular problem. The entire success of brainstorming depends on people feeling relaxed and uninhibited. If you're worried about looking like a fool in front of your boss or colleagues you will never have the confidence to brainstorm properly. A failed brainstorming session is miserable and destructive breeding nothing but frustration, anger and resentment. Be warned – make sure your colleagues are up to the task before you try this.

Laughing
'An Englishman, an Irishman and a Scottishman walk into a bar. The barman says 'is this some kind of joke?!'

Believe it or not, laughing at that joke would have required activity from five different areas of your brain at the same time.

UNDER PRESSURE

While it is clear that creativity can be encouraged through relaxation, it is equally viable for ideas to flow in a rather unpredictable fashion while an individual is exposed to stress. Unfortunately, the idea has taken hold that in order to be creative, all you have to do is sit around dreaming all day. If only this were true! The bad news is that for much of the time, people will want you to produce bright ideas in a hurry. The good news is that this pressure can be quite stimulating and often works in your favour. Sometimes when you simply have to produce an answer within a certain time you find that you can do it.

Some people thrive on this sort of pressure. In media careers such as journalism, broadcasting or advertising, working under pressure is quite normal. Often, if you are given a long time to complete a task, you find that instead of using the time to produce a beautiful and original piece of work, you either turn to more pressing matters and go back to the original task only when it has become urgent.

The puzzles that follow are deliberately designed to be stressful. You won't have nearly as much time as you would like to complete them. Even so, try to stick to the deadlines and surprise yourself with how much you can get done in the time available.

VI Lenin

After his death, Lenin's brain was studied and found to have
an abnormally large and numerous neurons in a particular region
that may explain his "strikingly acute and penetrating
mental processes" for which he was famous.

FIVE-MINUTE CHALLENGE

This is a little test to see how much you can accomplish when put under pressure of time. The three tasks below are not hard, but you have only five minutes to solve all of them.

Beheadings
In each case you have to cut the first letter off a common word to produce another.

1. Behead a piece of furniture to get 'talented'.
2. Behead a structure to get 'everything'.
3. Behead a murmur to get 'an absolute'.
4. Behead violently thrown to get 'an organ of the body'.
5. Behead a light to get 'a speaker'.
6. Behead a weed to get 'a devotee'.
7. Behead a fruit to get 'variety'.
8. Behead a boy's name to get 'status'.
9. Behead a noise to get 'an old boat'.
10. Behead an insult to get 'a relative'.
11. Behead a colour to get 'a liquid'.
12. Behead a fabric to get 'a kind'.

Answer on page 168.

Albert Einstein
Einstein's brain was similar in size to other humans except in the region that is responsible for math and spatial perception. In that region, his brain was 35% wider than average.

CREATIVITY FROM CONFUSION

In everyday life, the mind behaves rather like a strict and humourless teacher put in charge of a group of boisterous children. It forces us to think in a rather plodding, one-thing-at-a-time kind of way, for if the children (our thoughts) are not kept under control they will run about the place screaming, shouting and making a mess.

This might be a lot of fun, but it would interfere with everyday tasks such as driving a car or washing the dishes. For much of the time, we need to be in control of our thoughts and get them to carry out a variety of important tasks. The problem comes when we need to be creative. Creativity does not flourish in this environment. We need a way to break down the strictures that keep the rational mind under control and allow it to romp around and have a little fun. One way to do this is to make use of the power of chaos. This means using a number of methods to randomize information and give us a chance to make unusual connections that would be invisible in our normal mode of thinking.

FREE ASSOCIATION

This technique was originally used by psychoanalysis as a way of helping patients uncover their suppressed anxieties. It works well, however, as a means of liberating the conscious mind from all sorts of constraints. It is best to use a tape recorder to keep a record of each session. Start by sitting comfortably. You may want to close your eyes if that helps you to concentrate. Now, say the first word that pops into your mind. Quickly, without giving yourself any time to make rational connections, say another word, and another and another. Keep this up for as long as you wish. At first, you may find that you are a bit inhibited but, as you get used to the technique, you will find it easier to let your tongue run free and say things that you didn't intend it to say. After each session, listen to the tape several times and look out for interesting connections.

This technique has various applications. For example, if you are a writer, you could use it as a way of liberating your mind to allow characters and plot lines to develop. Alternatively, you can do this as part of a problem-solving strategy. Start with a word associated with the problem, and let your mind freewheel. You may find that you come up with words that suggest a solution. There is also a more general benefit: over time, you will begin to see patterns emerge that tell you something about the way your thought processes habitually work. This is a useful form of self-exploration that will help to deepen your understanding of your own motives and anxieties.

CREATIVE COLLAGE

This technique works well for those involved in various types of artistic creativity. Collect together a large assortment of pictures cut from magazines. You can also use all sorts of interesting odds and ends, for example a seashell, an odd-shaped stone, a brass electrical fitting or an old bottle stopper. Find a piece of board. Now comes the fun bit: arranging your materials on the board. Try lots of different arrangements until you find one that is really striking. When you are happy with your collage, stick everything in place.

Making a collage is a good way to relax and get yourself into a creative state of mind. If you examine the collage carefully, you may also find that you have unconsciously expressed thoughts and feelings that you can press into use as part of a creative project. And if you are really pleased with your effort, frame it and put it on the wall, give it to a friend or even sell it.

New connections
Every time you recall a memory or have a new thought,
you are creating a new connection in your brain.

RANDOMIZING

Many creative people suffer the frustration of not being able to break out of their normal mode of thought to embrace the creative notions that seem to hover all around them.

In the early twentieth century, some writers experimented with breaking down the formal structure of their text. The theory was that once text was liberated, new connections would be perceived. The technique involved taking pages of text, cutting them up and then reassembling them in a random order. Naturally, our commonsense mind will dismiss the randomized text as mere nonsense deprived of all meaning. Enthusiasts for the technique argued that it created a new and more vibrant text that was full of previously undiscovered meanings. Why not try it? The technique need not be confined to works of fiction. You can take any sort of text and randomize it in this way to see whether it throws up new meanings.

IDEA SHUFFLING

This is a rather less radical technique. It works best if you use a program such as Microsoft PowerPoint, but you can also use a word-processing program or even, if you are not comfortable with computers, pieces of blank card. Start by jotting down ideas at random. Do not make any attempt to evaluate your ideas at this stage. If using PowerPoint, create a new slide for each idea. This part of the process may take anything from a few minutes to many weeks. When you feel that you have enough ideas to work with, you can start to shuffle them about.

PowerPoint allows you to show all your slides at once and then move them around. If you are word processing, you can cut and paste text to create a similar effect. Soon, you will start to see themes emerge. Now you can start to evaluate your ideas, promoting the strong ones to a more prominent position and relegating others to the bottom of the heap. This is the most important part of the process, because this is where you decide the shape of the finished product. Don't hurry to reach a conclusion and rearrange your ideas as much as you like. Have the confidence to make bold creative decisions. If you decide to try something really radical, always save a copy of the current layout before making huge alterations. That way, if you later decide that your bright idea was a failure, you can always revert to the earlier version without having lost anything.

Eventually, you will end up with an outline that satisfies you. No matter how much you like the outline you've created, never regard it as set in stone. The essence of creativity is to allow ideas to develop and change freely throughout the process. So as you start putting your project together, consider the outline as fluid and still open to change.

CREATIVE TIP
Always keep stirring the pot. Good ideas will float to the surface unpredictably, but for that to happen there has to be plenty of thought and action going on.

FAMOUS BRAINS

Sir Isaac Newton (1643–1727)

Sir Isaac Newton was a clever man. Indeed, it was him who first observed and calculated the laws of gravity – the most thrilling advancement in science, for as we all know now, gravity is what connects the vastness of the universe. Newton also developed the laws on motion, principles of momentum and is even credited with the phrase 'standing on the shoulders of giants', which was said as a mocking insult to philosopher Robert Hooke who was short and hunchbacked.

USING CHAOS TO CREATE A PLOT

During creative writing classes, there is one exercise that always proves popular. It involves making up a story that uses a set of words. Try it yourself. Your plotline must also include the following:

- A missed opportunity.
- Mistaken identity.
- Something hidden.
- A shocking turn of events.
- Sibling rivalry.

There are no right answers to this exercise; just make sure that you use all the words and plot elements you've been given. When you've done it once, see whether you can do it again using a different plot. You might also find that it's fun to try the exercise in a group.

PORTRAIT   TRUCK   SINGING   BLEARY   CONFIDENCE
CERTAINTY   ROMANTIC   HAPPY   POLICE   VALUABLE
FLOWERS   UNAWARE   PHILOSOPHER   BELL   DIAMOND
FRANTIC   AMMUNITION   CHOCOLATE   WELCOME   REPAIR
CALCULATOR   BORDER   BALANCE   GRANDMOTHER
CONFIDENCE   FORTUNE   FADED   RABBIT   SANDWICH
CARPENTER   CREATION

CHAOS CONTROLLED

AIM Many of our creativity tasks have involved coaxing flashes of inspiration to rise up out of the subconscious. This is sometimes all you need, but frequently the conscious mind plays a vital role in organizing this material into a useful form. That is what this task is all about.

TASK Start by setting yourself a task. It could be writing a story, solving a problem, planning some job around the house or anything else that requires creative input. Phase one involves jotting down all your ideas just as they come to you. Don't worry about creating a logical order at this stage. Just chuck everything down higgledy-piggledy. A computer is useful for this sort of thing but, if you don't have one, a sheet of paper will be fine.

Phase two involves trying to organize your thoughts in broad sections. This will give your project a structure or framework on which you can put the fine detail. Trying to martial your original thoughts into sections will inevitably lead to discarding some of your ideas as useless but it will also lead you on to new ones. You might find as you go on that you need to rename and re-order your sections so that your ideas make better sense.

The detailed work begins in phase three. Within each section organize your ideas logically so they flow in a way that makes perfect sense. This is especially important if your project is of the type that needs to be communicated to others.

This entire process is one of the re-organizing and refining your ideas until you have produced the clearest and most complete statement possible of what you are trying to achieve.

HELP
Even when you have your project supposedly finished, always leave some room for the element of serendipity or happy accident. Your creative mind doesn't stop working just because you have consciously put everything in order. Be prepared at the last minute to dispense with some things and put new material in if you have a flash of inspiration. Usually these last minute changes are the things that turn your work into something special.

LIBIDO AND MORTIDO

Sex and creativity have had a long and steamy affair. (Renoir famously remarked, 'I paint with my prick'!) The relationship between the two appears blatantly in many paintings, sculptures, novels, films and plays with a sexual theme.

But it appears much more subtly in the way in which creative people are affected by their work. The act of creation seems closely linked, at some unconscious level, with the act of procreation. To put it at its crudest, creative people get a sexual buzz from their work. This is one reason they are, quite literally, passionate about what they are doing. Their deep commitment to their work echoes the commitment one feels for a lover. Furthermore, in the post-Freudian age, we know that both consciously and unconsciously people may express their deepest feelings through their creative work. This creative urge is normally called 'libido'. Libido also describes sexual desire.

Love hormones and autism
Oxytocin, one of the hormones responsible for triggering feelings of love in the brain, has shown some benefits to helping control repetitive behaviors in those with autism.

DESTRUCTIVE URGES

It is often overlooked, however, that according to Freud, libido has a partner. This is the destructive death instinct called 'mortido'. Psychologically, there has always been controversy over whether mortido actually exists. Do we really have a mental component that urges us towards death? In some cultures, this idea is accepted without question. In India, for example, the dance of Shiva expresses both the creative and destructive urges simultaneously.

Why should destruction be important creatively? Because it gives us the urge to tear up that which is old and out of date, and to make something new in its place. It also gives us the courage to junk work that is not up to standard and strive to make something better.

There is a well-known Japanese story about a potter who finished a piece of work, placed it in the middle of her studio, burned incense and contemplated it. Day after day, she examined the new work from every angle. Then, after some weeks, she came to a decision. She fetched a hammer and smashed the new work to pieces. To do such a thing required a huge amount of courage and dedication. It would have been easier for her to accept the piece (and probably no one would have said anything because she was a very famous artist). But in the end, she could not accept work that was not up to her very high standards.

Learning to smash things that need smashing is a part of creativity that is often overlooked. It is very easy to accept what we have made, but it is far more difficult to have the courage to destroy things. It is also easy to accept the work of others and not make waves by criticizing it. But mortido urges us to smash up what is second rate and to do away with anything that has served its turn, and if we are to be truly creative, this is a lesson we must learn.

Brain death
The brain can live for 4 to 6 minutes without oxygen,
and then it begins to die. No oxygen for 5 to 10 minutes
will result in permanent brain damage.

THE DOORS OF PERCEPTION

Books on creativity tend to avoid the role drugs and alcohol have played in the lives of many creative people. This is entirely understandable as no one wants to appear to be condoning or encouraging behaviour that is unwise or even illegal. But to dodge the issue would be just plain dishonest.

A list of all the creative people who have become notorious for their reliance on booze and illegal substances would make a very long chapter all on its own. Another list of lives ruined or brought to an untimely end would be almost as long. This is by no means a recent phenomenon. The Chinese poet Li Po, who lived during the T'ang dynasty (618–906), was famous for his love affair with the bottle and eventually drowned while drunkenly trying to embrace a reflection of the moon in the waters of the Yangtse river. There has been no shortage of creative types eager to follow his example.

What is the special attraction that drugs hold for creative people? First, there is the task of breaking down the barrier between the normal everyday mind and the creative force that lies hidden in the unconscious. This is and always has been an enormous problem. People have tried all sorts of methods to liberate the mind and allow the creative force to flow. Without question drugs do help to get rid of inhibitions and, in many cases, they allow users to see things that would normally lie hidden. They also conjure up fantasies of such power and beauty that they can seem like divine revelations. For people who spend much of their lives struggling to force the unconscious to yield its secrets, the prospect of a quick means of achieving this aim is very seductive.

Second, creative work often involves examining life far more closely than most of us would dare to do. Our life is a great mystery and it is the mission of creative people to explore that mystery in as many ways as possible. Sometimes, however, that exploration leads people along dark and dangerous paths. Life can seem unbearably bleak and those who examine this aspect too closely often come to harm. In these circumstances drugs may offer a temporary respite from an overdose of reality. In reality, of course, the drugs themselves only exacerbate the problem.

At one time the use of drugs to enhance creativity involved only occasional use by a few isolated individuals. If we look back to the nineteenth century, for example, we find people such as Samuel Taylor Coleridge who famously saw a vision while under the influence of opium that he tried to capture in his poem Kubla Khan. As long as drug use was the vice of a few eccentrics it was a very minor danger. In the early 1950s, however, the British writer Aldous Huxley experimented with mescalin, a drug capable of producing psychedelic experiences. What happened to him is described in his essay entitled The Doors of Perception (the title came from the poet William Blake who said, 'If the doors of perception were cleansed every thing would appear to man as it is, infinite. For man has closed himself up, till he sees all things thru' narrow chinks of his cavern'). Huxley's work had a huge influence on the '60s generation; in fact the band The Doors chose their name as a direct reference to his essay.

Suddenly there was a drug explosion. The taking of drugs was seen not just as a recreational activity but as an easily accessible route to higher levels of consciousness. No matter how much politicians, police and parents disapproved, the younger generation felt they had found something wonderful that could transform their lives for the better. They were encouraged in this belief by older people like Dr Timothy Leary who memorably told them to, 'Turn on, tune in and drop out.'

The fact that drugs were extremely dangerous made no difference to their popularity. Famous names of that generation such as Jimi Hendrix and Janis Joplin may have died as a result of their drug use but that did nothing to persuade the younger generation to give them up and that attitude has not only persisted by flourished. Now the Western world has a huge drug problem that simply cannot be solved. Although there is a constant call for tougher and tougher sentences on drug dealers and users, there is in fact nothing that will deter a huge number of people from abusing substances.

Here we are not concerned with the moral or legal aspects of drug taking but only with its effect on creativity. The central question we need to ask is, 'Does taking drugs make you more creative?' There are countless musicians, painters, poets and writers who would say it does. The evidence, however, is not compelling. Looking back at the '60s it is hard to see anything worthwhile that was added to creative thought by drug use. The pretty psychedelic patterns have faded now and much of the music has been forgotten.

Drugs and alcohol make people feel that they are being creative but, sadly, any insights are fleeting and do not translate readily into any form that can be expressed by art. On the other hand the effects of drug use on health are all too easily seen. Not only do young people still die as a result of drug use, but some of those who survived the '60s are visibly damaged by their past excesses. So, if you want to be creative, don't do drugs.

1899
Aspirin was marketed as a pain reliever, but was not available without a prescription until 1915.

'Genius is one per cent *inspiration* and ninety-nine per cent **perspiration**.'

Thomas Edison, inventor (1847–1931)

CHAPTER 4

MEMORY DEVELOPMENT TRICKS

'The advantage of a **bad memory**
is that one enjoys several times
the same *good things* for the first time.'
Friedrich Nietzsche

SHORT TERM
MEMORY TIPS

Up until the 1950s scientists thought we just had one mechanism for memory – the brain tried to store as much as it could from the vast amount of information that is programmed into it. However, since then scientists have discovered that the brain uses several means of remembering information for varying lengths of time.

Our short-term memories deal with two types of facts:
1. Trivia: the colour of the trousers of the man in front of you in the queue this morning. This type of knowledge will mostly prove to be useless but the brain stores it in case it is of value.
2. Specific task information: the driving route you must take to reach an important meeting. This type of information is at the forefront of your mind while you are doing it, but once it is completed the information becomes irrelevant.

The short term memory works by virtue of three distinct mechanisms in the brain:
1. Phonological loop – this processes words and sounds
2. Visuo-spatial sketchpad – this registers images.
3. Central executive – this combines the words, sounds and images into a single thought.

THE STATE OF THE ART

How good is your memory right now? The following pages will seek to assess the current state of your memory with a series of tests that increase in difficulty. Just use whatever memory methods you normally use; it really doesn't matter if you do badly. The idea of this section is to show you just how much you can improve your memory by putting into practice the techniques taught later in the book.

SHORT-TERM MEMORY TASK 1

The 'Flurble' test
TIME 3 minutes **LEVEL** Easy

Instructions

1. Study the six pictures with strange names.
2. Spend three minutes memorizing them.
3. Now close the book, draw all six objects and write the correct names beneath them.
4. Check your answers against the original pictures.
5. Now spend a further five minutes memorizing the original pictures.
6. Leave this exercise and then tomorrow, without further memorizing, try to draw and name what you can recall.

SPLINK

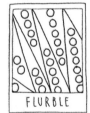
VLOOM

GRUNDER

FLURBLE

SLERT

TRUMPLE

How did you do?

Although memory is always capable of improvement, if you were able to draw and name all six pictures on both occasions, your short-term memory is working well.

SHORT-TERM MEMORY TASK 2

It happened last Friday
TIME 3 minutes   **LEVEL** Easy

Here's another easy test of your short-term memory. All you have to do is read through the passage below. You can study it as hard as you like for three minutes, then cover the story and answer the questions:

Last Friday, Jim's wife, Sandra, asked him to go to the shops and buy some things ready for her parents' visit at the weekend. She needed a couple of pizza bases, some canned tomatoes, mozzarella and a couple of bottles of wine. She told him to go to Brown's because it was cheaper than Thompson's (and anyway Tommy Brown was her cousin). She told him to stop on the way back and get the car cleaned, and to pick up their twins, Mark and Michael, from school. Jim was almost home when he discovered that he'd forgotten the cheese, so he went back to town. This time he went to Thompson's, because it wasn't as far to drive. He also bought a bag of pretzels and some salted peanuts because he remembered that his father-in-law, Dick, liked them.

Questions
1. What is Jim's father-in-law called?
2. Which shop does his wife tell him to go to?
3. What does he forget on his first attempt?
4. Why does he go to Thompson's rather than Brown's on his second trip?
5. What are the names of Jim's twins?
6. Where is he supposed to pick them up?
7. What is Jim's wife called?
8. How many bottles of wine is Jim supposed to buy?
9. What canned goods does Jim's wife ask him to get?
10. What is he supposed to do with the car?
11. When are his wife's parents due to visit?
12. What is the connection between his wife and the owner of Brown's?
13. What sort of cheese does Jim forget to buy?
14 What does he buy specifically for his father-in-law?
15. On which day does the story take place?

SHORT-TERM MEMORY TASK 3

Kim's game

TIME 30 seconds   **LEVEL** Easy

Here's a more difficult task to test your visual memory. In Rudyard Kipling's book Kim, the young hero was trained in observation by being told to look at a tray full of objects and then, when the tray was removed, he had to remember as many of them as possible. Kim's game has long been a favourite at parties but it also has a serious role in memory training. There are 8 objects pictured on this page. Your job is to look at them for 30 seconds and try to fix as many as possible in your mind. Then, with the book closed, write a list of what you can remember. If you don't get all the objects first time – and you'd have to have a very good memory to do that – you can have another go (and another) until you get the whole lot. And then try again, but this time double the amount of objects you'll need to remember, doubling the time as you do so. And then double it again.

DON'T PANIC!

You won't be able to bring things to mind if you are in a panic. Give yourself time and work calmly.
(If you're revising for a test or exam, start in plenty of time and don't try to do it all the night before.)

Blinking

Each time we blink, our brain kicks in and keeps things illuminated so the whole world doesn't go dark each time we blink (about 20,000 times a day)

STUDYING AND RECALL

If, in spite of all the advice in this book, you find some facts just won't stick in your mind, take time to work out why. If they are too boring, use wild and wacky associations to make them more memorable. Really childish humour works wonders. But if you still get no result, consider why you cannot remember. Is your subconscious telling you that you're studying the wrong course?

Does the material that you're trying to remember have bad associations that you aren't acknowledging?

LONG TERM
MEMORY TIPS

Many of you probably believe that you have poor long term memory. For instance, you probably debated only recently something like the name of a hotel you stayed in on a significant holiday. You won't have been able to recall it but then, a few days later, while listening to a song the name will pop into your head. (The song will have been one you listened to during the holiday.) So you had remembered it, you just couldn't recall it. These 'triggers' like the music are very helpful in recalling latent memories.

The factors involved in the quality of long term memory are:

1. **Vividness** – how clear in your mind is the original experience? Do you recall it with absolute certainty, as if it were yesterday, or do you suspect the memory has been 'planted' there based on conversations you have had about it?

2. **Frequency** – how often do you recall the event? Daily, or once every few years at family gatherings?

3. **Ageing process** – everyone's memory gets poorer as we get older. It's a fact of life.

4. **Interference** – when the memory of recent event muddles or replaces the original memory. For example, you might recall bumping into an old friend on a train journey to work. But if you travel on the same train every day you will probably struggle to identify the specific day it occurred. If however, you encountered the same friend while on your annual holiday, the memory will be more clear.

THE LONG AND WINDING ROAD

This is an exercise in using your long-term memory. There is nothing you need to do to form this type of memory – it happens automatically. Your unconscious will simply file stuff away without any reference to your conscious desires at all. This can be quite inconvenient. Sometimes you may find yourself desperate to remember an incident from long ago, only to find that you can't dredge it up. At other times, you'll find yourself plagued with memories that are either quite useless and distracting or, even worse, decidedly unpleasant.

What to do? It is a good idea, every now and again, to deliberately stimulate long-term memory. There are several ways of doing this and you should use all of them. One is simply to sit and recollect incidents from your past. You can just ramble aimlessly down memory lane if you want to, or you can pick out a specific train of thought (schooldays, jobs you have held, old friends, former lovers, whatever takes your fancy). Just let your mind meander where it will. The more relaxed you feel, the more likely you are to have a good experience. An extra way of stimulating the flow of memory is to either write your thoughts down (you don't have to be an expert writer, notes will do just as well), or to recount your experiences to a relative or friend. If you do use someone as a recipient for memories, make sure it is a person who is both willing and trustworthy.

Another way to get the long-term memory centre working is to look through mementoes and photographs, or to visit places that you used to frequent long ago. This is obviously a very powerful stimulant and you'll probably find that once you do it the flow of memory will turn into a flood.

Finally, you might try talking to friends, relatives, colleagues and acquaintances form your past. People are often very keen to do this (as can be seen from the success of various websites that encourage people to get back in contact with their former friends).

For most people, there are considerable benefits in keeping their long-term memory in good repair. It aids mental health by reinforcing our sense of identity, reassuring us about who we are and how we fit into our own personal life story. It can provide a feeling of warmth and security that is far better than anything you can get from pills.

Just one word of warning – if your life is full of unresolved conflicts, unhappy memories and repressed traumas, you should only carry out this exercise in the company of a trained professional.

To help you begin your journey, try the suggestions below. They will give you some preliminary thoughts that will launch your voyage of exploration in the right direction. We tried a questionnaire a bit like this earlier in the book, but this one is more ambitious and, as you are doing it entirely for your own private interest, you should take your time over it and not let yourself feel rushed.

Considering these questions will almost certainly put you in a mood where other memories come flooding out. This mood of reverie may persist for hours or even days.

1. Write down or talk about your very favourite memory. With luck, you will have lots of good ones to choose from, and deciding which is the best will be part of the fun. Examining memories will also set off trains of thought that you will find interesting and rewarding.

2. Discuss, with yourself or others, who is the one person in your life you would like to meet again. Why is that person so important to you? Recall as many events associated with that person as you can. Once you start, you will find other memories begin to push forward into your consciousness.

3. List your greatest achievements. These need not be grand – you don't have to have climbed Everest or explored the Amazon rainforest. Little things will do as long as they mean a lot to you.

4. Name a favourite TV programme from when you were a child. Remember as many details as you can. Just what was it you enjoyed so much/ Would you still enjoy it now if you were able to see a re-run?

5. Write something about pets you had in the past. Pet memories are often sweet and sad at the same time. They are also a very potent reminder of times past.

6. Discuss someone you knew who changed (or failed to change) the course of your life. What would you say to that person if you met him or her today?

7. Think of the five things you remember best about your parents. Parent memories are, of course, some of our most powerful. Handle with care!

8. What was the best job you ever had? And the worst? Did you follow the career you wanted? Have you enjoyed your working life or are there things you would have done differently?

9. What scene from your past would you most like to visit again? If you could, would you change anything or was it so perfect that you'd like to live it all, over again?

10. Think of a day from the distant past in as much detail as you possibly can. Don't just remember people and events, but conjure up memories of things, colours, textures and smells.

Neocortex
The neocortex makes up about 76% of the human brain
and is responsible for language and consciousness. The human
neocortex is much larger than in animals.

LONG-TERM MEMORY TASK

The good old days

Here's another test of your long-term memory. This is one area where older people tend to excel. Youngsters, whose brains are firing on all cylinders may, even so, find it harder to recall the distant past than their elders.

1. What was your grandmother's full name?
2. What was the address of the house you were born in?
3. What was your first cuddly toy called?
4. What was your favourite meal when you were a child?
5. What was your nickname at your first school?
6. What did you grandfather do for a living?
7. What did your grandfather look like?
8. Think of a present that you were given when you were under five years old.
9. Visualize the house you grew up in. What colour was the front door?
10. Who lived next door to you when you were little?
11. Can you picture your first day at school? What did you wear?
12. Who was your first teacher?
13. What was the naughtiest thing you did when you were little?
14. What is your earliest memory?
15. Who did you sit next to in school when you were eleven years old?
16. Which teacher did you really dislike intensely?
17. Can you still remember any poem, speech or reading you learnt by heart at school?
18. Who was the first person you had a crush on?
19. Who was the first person you dated?
20. Who first broke your heart?
21. Who was your best friend when you were eleven?
22. What is the first holiday you remember?
23. What are your earliest memories of Christmas (or other appropriate religious holiday)?
24. Describe a favourite toy.
25. When did you learn to ride a bike?
26. Who taught you to swim?

27. Who was your first real friend?
28. What was your favourite childhood game?
29. What was your favourite TV programme when you were five?
30. What was the first record you ever bought?
31. What was your nickname at school?
32. Do you have sharp pictures in your mind of events from the distant past?
33. Is there a smell that brings back particularly vivid memories for you?
34. What was your first pet called?
35. How many of your cuddly toys can you name?
36. Can you recall any of your birthday parties (below the age of eleven) in detail?
37. What was your favourite song when you were under five?
38. Did you have a gang when you were under eleven? Who else was in it?
39. Can you remember any near misses you had as a kid (such as a road accident)?
40. What was your most serious childhood illness?
41. Do you have one favourite memory (from your whole life)?
42. Is there one childhood friend you long to meet again?
43. Can you still remember stuff like science formulae that you learnt for exams?
44. Do you remember times long past more easily than recent events?
45. Can you remember where you were when you heard of the death of Diana, Princess of Wales?

HOW DID YOU DO?

The majority of people will have done well in this test and answered over 30 of the questions. What's more, it is likely that as you started to answer the questions, you were prompted to remember more and more. This mood of reverie may persist for quite some time. It might even prompt you to do things such as getting out old photos and souvenirs, phoning old acquaintances, or even trying to trace people you have lost touch with. Once you stimulate long-term memory, it becomes hugely powerful. You may well be startled at the amount of detail you store in your memory. I have found that just writing out the questions has released a powerful set of images from my childhood, and I can smell creosote on old wood heated in the sunshine – a smell I always associated with summer as a child.

Blood
Your brain uses 20% of the blood circulating in your body.

MNEMONICS

Frameworks and patterns reinforce the neurological pathways in our brains to make memories stronger. This fact leads to a range of techniques which can be very helpful when you need to remember details, facts, sequences and so on. Mnemonics are simple tricks used to stimulate memory and help a person remembers facts or lists. They can be verbal, visual, kinaesthetic or auditory.

Mnemonics is named after the Greek goddess of memory Mnemosyne. Among the first people to use the system was the Greek poet Simonides in the sixth century BC, and many people who perform amazing memory stunts today still use the method credited to him. Try these tasks to help you get to grips with mnemonics.

PEGWORDS

This is a system whereby you can recall ten or more memorable words, facts or whatever. A useful tool for students studying for exams. Essentially you associate each word or fact with a number which rhymes with it (or has some other obvious association.) The numbers therefore become pegs on which to hang the things you want to remember. Once you have worked out your list spend as much time as you need memorizing it.

For example: one/gun; two/who; three/free; four/poor – you get the idea.

Then, when you have a list of items to remember, you use each number to prompt your recall of detailed information. For instance, the number 4 (poor), could help you remember vital information about the English Poor Laws for your history exam. Once you get to grips with mnemonics you will discover its great potential.

Acronyms
This technique uses initial letters of the actual things you want to remember and make a word from them. If you are British you probably learned the colours of the rainbow (Red, Orange, Yellow, Green, Blue, Indigo, Violet) by

the initials of 'Richard Of York Gives Battle In Vain'. If you're North American perhaps you learned the names of the Great Lakes as HOMES (Huron, Ontario, Michigan, Erie, Superior). You may also have learned to spell 'necessary' as Never Eat Cake Eat Salmon Sandwiches And Remain Young.

This technique can be applied to anything in your daily working life. For instance, if you are bad at remembering people's names (which can be especially embarrassing at work) think up an acronym for those who attend the monthly sales meeting. By rearranging the order of Larry, Eric, Andy, Neil, Elizabeth, Peter, Hal and Tricia you can produce ELEPHANT.

Cranial nerves

Here is a bit of technical information that you will probably never need, but it will serve as a good test of your powers of recall. Listed below you will find the 12 cranial nerves and your task is to construct a mnemonic that helps you to remember them in the order given. First, divide them into groups of three. (Note that in each group I have put the shortest name first and the longest last, as this will help you.) Now make up your own mnemonic to memorize the 12 names.

OPTIC   OLFACTIVE
COMMON OCULAR MOTOR

PATHETIC   TRIGEMINAL
EXTERNAL OCULAR MOTOR

FACIAL   AUDITORY
GLOSSO-PHARYNGEAL

SPINAL   HYPOGLOSSOL
PNEUMOGASTRIC

'I developed a system of mnemonics for improving my
memory and then discovered that the Greeks had been doing
exactly the same thing 2,000 years ago.'
Dominic O'Brien, first World Memory Champion

RITUAL

Memorization is simply a matter of making something stick in your mind. How do you make something stick? You use glue, of course! Memory is just another sort of glue. In fact, it is many sorts and, because you want to remember things for different amounts of time, you need different strengths of glue. Repeating something over and over again until it is firmly lodged in your mind is one of the less sophisticated glues you can use, but useless nonetheless.

For some people, the very best way to learn about something is to go and do it. They get more information from that than they would from any amount of book learning. This ability lends itself to a whole area of memory techniques based on doing.

When I was young, I went to a school that had strong views about pupils bringing the right books and equipment with them for lessons. The words, 'Sorry, I forgot', were not met with a smile. So, how did I manage to avoid trouble? I constructed a ritual for filling my school bag every evening. It was very complicated, but that was precisely the reason it worked. Not only did each book and item of equipment have its own place, but everyone had to be put in the bag in the correct order. It soon became a virtual impossibility to forget anything, because if I did, the ritual didn't feel right and I'd soon spot my oversight.

That is one sort of ritual, but there are other much more complicated and useful ones.

When something that we do regularly is considered important, one way of making sure it all goes to plan is to turn it into ritual. Churches have been good at this for centuries. So have other institutions such as monarchies. A nice bit of ritual binds the community together and reminds everyone of their place in the grand scheme. But how is this relevant to your quest for a better memory?

The army is often derided for teaching people to do things by numbers. But this is actually a very good and practical use of ritual. How else would you teach a youngster who has little formal education (and may not be too bright) to strip down a complicated device such as a machine gun, correct a jammed mechanism, and put it all back together again, without losing any of the pieces? Ritual, that's how. Once they learn to do it by numbers, they will never forget, even when under fire and in a highly stressed state. It has become impossible to leave out one of the numbered stages.

My wife has another sort of ritual. When she visits the supermarket she always makes exactly the same tour. Most of us buy more or less the same stuff each week, but with some changes (for example, you probably don't need razors every week). But once you've committed the order to memory, you no longer have to think about it and can concentrate your energy on remember any changes to the usual routine (for example, maybe this week you fancy wine instead of beer). You can extend your ritual to cover not just the supermarket, but all the other places you normally have to visit. The ritual makes it very unlikely you'll forget anything important. Some people might object that shopping this way is rather boring and mechanical. To counter that, we save the fun stuff (new clothes, CDs, etc.) until last so that we can enjoy them at our leisure.

Don't knock ritual! It is an effortless way to remember complicated information without mistakes. Think, for example, of how you drive a manual car. Do you consciously think: apply brakes, slow down, change gear, check mirror, look both ways at junction? No, of course you don't. Once you can drive, the whole process becomes automatic. No matter what the circumstances on the road, the appropriate ritual will cut in. The only time you'll be flummoxed is if you get into a violent skid and haven't bothered to learn the technique for dealing with a skid.

ORDER, ORDER!

When you learn a list of things (telephone numbers, for example) make sure that you frequently change the order in which you rehearse them. If you don't, there is a strong risk that you will be committing the order itself to memory. If that happens, you will find that you have to go through the whole list every time you want to find one item. So, when you rehearse your list, mix it up so that the order never forms part of your memory pattern.

RITUAL

AIM A memory ritual is a set of actions, the more bizarre the better, designed to remind you of something important you must do.

TASK My elder cousin used to remind herself to wake up at a certain time by programming her body clock with a ritual. As she went to bed she'd turn around three times while tapping herself three times on the head at each turn and repeating out loud the time at which she wanted to wake. Your task is to construct a ritual that will remind you of some important event of your choice. In order to work efficiently the ritual should be strange enough to embed itself in your unconscious and prompt your memory at the appropriate time.

White matter
The white matter is made up of dendrites and axons,
which create the network by which neurons send their signals..

HELP
Why go to all this trouble when you could set an alarm clock?
Well, memory is like a muscle, the more you use it the stronger it gets. By relying on machines or written notes we weaken our power to remember. If you make a habit of giving your memory a workout it will continue to look after you even when you get older.

MUSICAL MEMORIES

Many people like to use music as a background to any sort of work. Runners in the park, kids doing homework, works on assembly lines and shoppers in supermarkets all receive a daily dose of background music. Indeed, much has been written about the so-called 'Mozart effect' – the IQs of children boosted by listening to the composer – but does the music help or distract?

This is a very grey area. The only thing I would absolutely advise against, when trying to memorize, is having a TV on anywhere near you. If you can see it, you will not be able to concentrate on the work in hand. Even the most witless game show or soap looks entrancing when the alternative is to do some work. If you can only hear the TV, it's not much better – you'll be wondering, even if only at the back of your mind, what is happening on screen. You'll almost certainly give in at some point and go to take a quick peek. You may return to your work (or not), but in any case your concentration will be broken.

Music is far more a matter of personal taste. My kids swear that they can revise to the strains of heavy rock. I'm sure that you can do some tasks to music but I doubt that you can marshal all your concentration when you are listening to something loud and lively. Having said that, I must confess that I'm writing this to the strains of Pink Floyd, and my concentration is unbroken so far.

So how about classical music? Like many people, I enjoy popular classics. I can happily listen to The Four Seasons or Scheherazade, but it's not the sort of music I'd choose to work to – until recently, that is. I read an article about the way in which classical music (any classical music) could increase your concentration and improve memory. Since it was strictly relevant to this book I gave it a try and, to my surprise, it worked very well indeed. I recommend it to you. You don't even have to like the music. But it does create a calm atmosphere where you will find concentration easier and where memories will stick. And the quicker you learn, the sooner you can get back to the TV.

Don't just memorize at odd moments. Plan a session, decide how long it will last and what you will achieve. Decide when you will take a rest.

TUNING IN 1

AIM This is a very strong memory technique that should only be used for information that you want to retain indefinitely. As a teenager I made the mistake of memorizing all my physics formulas to tunes from popular classics. I now can't listen to certain pieces of music (Carmen in particular is a nightmare) without remembering useless information about Watts and Ohms.

TASK Simply set the information you want to recall to a well-known catchy tune. For the sake of experiment, here's a list of the planets in our solar system in their order from the sun. If you're British sing the list to the tune of God Save the Queen (Americans can use My Country 'Tis of Thee which is, of course, the same tune). This is how it goes:

Mercury, Venus, Earth

Mars, Jupiter, Saturn

Venus, Neptune, Pluto

You'll find the last line a bit of a tight fit but that doesn't matter. In fact, paradoxically, because the tune doesn't quite work it will be all the more memorable. My father taught me the alphabet to the tune of Twinkle, Twinkle Little Star. X, Y and Z don't work at all, which is one reason that bit was the easiest to remember.

HELP
Always choose a simple tune you know very well. This technique
is mental superglue, anything you learn this way is fixed for life,
so only use it for really important tasks.

REVISION TECHNIQUES

I f you find yourself unable to retain information, there may be several possible reasons. The main one is usually stress. You'll never be able to memorize if you let yourself get stressed. Memory is like sex – you have to be in the right mood, and that means feeling happy, relaxed and enthusiastic about what you are doing. This is very important for revision.

- Do NOT leave revising to the last minute. Start in good time and do a little – thoroughly – each day. It is far better to learn a little bit well than to try to cram in a whole lot and make a mess of it. To get it all done on time, you must plan your revision well.
- Do things to ensure you're in a good mood. Have some snacks and drinks (non-alcoholic) nearby to reward yourself for your efforts. If you like music, put some on at a low volume (you won't revise properly if you have to contend with loud music).
- Make sure that you are not too warm or too cold.
- Allow plenty of fresh air into the room. A stuffy room makes you drowsy and messes up your ability to concentrate.
- Keep other members of the family away and get someone to answer the phone and take message for you.
- To revise successfully, you need to concentrate for at least half an hour to an hour. Too little will do you no good and too much will make you stale. After each session, take a break. When you are revising hard for an exam, you can get in three or four one-hour sessions a day, then go out and do something completely different.

Trying to forget

One of the ways in which you differ from a computer is that your memories cannot be deleted at will. Memories that are not reviewed regularly will fade eventually. Memories that are of no further interest (like a once-only telephone number) will vanish without trace. Unpleasant memories have a habit of sticking just because they are unpleasant. The harder you struggle against such memories, the harder they are to erase. My uncle was with troops who liberated a Nazi death camp, and he struggled with the memory for the next forty years.

The only way (and it's by no means infallible) to deal with such memories is to review them when they resurface.

What's stopping you?

A major cause of faulty memory is lack of understanding. Certain things can be learnt parrot fashion, whether you understand them or not (though almost any attempt at memorization is improved by understanding). For example, you can learn the dates of all the battles in the American Civil War by rote if you want to. But how much better it would be if you understood the background, who was fighting and why. When you have that sort of framework to hang the information on, it is far easier to make it stick.

Some things just cannot be learnt without understanding them. Science without understanding becomes a jumble of weird symbols and figures. Literature becomes soulless and without meaning. If you master the background to a subject, the information will be easier to assimilate.

If you really can't remember, despite your best efforts, you need to ask yourself why. Are you studying something you really hate just to please your parents? Are you in a career that no longer interests you? Are you afraid of failing your exams? If there is some unresolved issue that is stopping you from memorizing successfully, then unless you face and resolve it, you will find your efforts constantly frustrated.

Largest brain

While an elephant's brain is larger than a human brain, the human brain is 2% of the total body weight (compared to just 0.15% of an elephant's brain). This means that humans have the largest brain to body size on the entire planet.

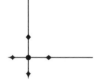

VISUALIZATION

Visualization is simply a technique whereby you create mental pictures. By doing this you can alter your mood in a number of important ways. First, you will learn to create calm, happy moods that will increase your inner peace. Second, by imagining how you will deal with a difficult situation, you can prepare yourself to handle it better. More controversially, many people believe that by visualizing a desired outcome, they can bring it about in reality.

Some people are born visualizers. Their imagination is full of vivid pictures and vibrant colours; others do not find it easy to think in pictures. Natural visualizers, for example, will automatically conjure up vivid and detailed pictures of settings and characters when they read a book. Or when a friend describes her holiday, a natural visualize will automatically create a vision of that place in their mind's eye. With practice, visualization can become an effortless process for everyone.

Visualizing is valuable because it allows us to experience vicariously situations that we are unable, for a variety of reasons, to experience at first hand. Those who perfect the technique often find that they can 'see' a solution to a problem even when they have been unable to discover it by the normal processes of reasoning.

Seven steps to visualization

The following steps show how to use visualization to assist in a creative project.

1. Choose a room where you can be quiet and feel comfortable.
2. Sit in a comfortable position, or lie down if you prefer. Relax. Have background music on if you find that it helps.
3. Close your eyes, and let your mind start to build a picture of the project you are working on.
4. The aim is to build the most detailed picture possible of your project. Try to see what it will look like when it is finished.
5. Don't spend time sorting out worries and problems. Those things can be dealt with elsewhere. This is the place for creating a positive vision that will encourage you in your efforts.

6. Make full use of your powers of imagination. For example, if you need expensive equipment, then as long as you can imagine it, you can have it.

7. Visualization is not magic. Some people are keen to believe that if you visualize a completed project it will in some magic way become reality. It won't. Visualization encourages you by providing a positive vision of what you can achieve, but it is never a substitute for action.

Basic Visualization

Some people have great visual imagination, while others have little or none. Here's a very easy exercise for those who are not quite sure which category they fall into. You should sit comfortably, close your eyes and imagine in as much detail as possible how you would carry out a very simple task like, for example, making a sandwich. Work at capturing every detail in your mind's eye. Get the bread out of the bread bin, look at its colour and texture, fetch the butter and sandwich filling from the fridge. Take a knife out and carefully spread the butter and then the filling. Place the top slice on the sandwich and cut the whole thing in half. Then picture yourself washing the knife and putting it back in the drawer. Did you make yourself feel so hungry that you needed a real sandwich afterwards? Success!

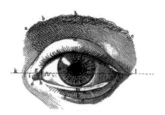

HELP

The success of visualization is in the detail. It is necessary to observe the things you want to visualize very closely (just as you would if you wanted to draw them) and then file away mental pictures of what they look like.

Memory Lane

Think of the street where you live (or any other street that you know really well). In your mind's eye, walk down the street depositing items that you want to remember in all the front gardens. You can include just about anything. In our illustration the man is reminding himself to take an umbrella when he goes to work (rain is forecast), get in a round of golf when he comes home, and buy butter, sugar and tea. There's a list of 'Things To Do' outside the local shop. Finally, he reminds himself to go to a friend's party where he will book tickets for Hawaii (his friend is in the travel business and gets him a discount).

You can extend this technique as much as you like. Some people, for example, learn dates by mentally carving them on a stone timeline. Another use for visual memory is in remembering faces and places. If visual memories work for you (there's no particular trick to doing it), you just have to remember to do it! If you're visiting a new town for the first time, make sure you keep a visual record of the route you take through the town so that you can find your way back to where you parked the car.

If I Were A Rich Man

AIM This technique is controversial but has many devotees who are convinced of its efficacy. It involves visualizing yourself in some situation that you deeply desire to experience for real. The theory is that, the more you visualize yourself achieving your aim, the easier it will be to bring about success in real life. My only comment is that, for the technique to stand any chance at all of working, your desire would need to be overwhelming.

TASK For the sake of argument, let's assume that you want to be rich (though the technique should work just as well with any other ambition you might have). Visualize every detail of your new life. What sort of house would you live in? What sort of car would you drive? What clothes would you wear? What holidays would you go on?

> **HELP**
> Don't forget that your new situation will have a down side.
> In life there is always a down side. Before you get too carried
> away you might like to work some of these negative aspects
> into your visualization.

Just A Perfect Day

AIM Visualization is useful because, if you can see a desired outcome in your
mind's eye, it is much easier to achieve such an outcome in reality. Some
people find this so easy that they do it naturally without any instruction,
but others find it very difficult. Anyone can achieve a degree of
proficiency if they practise hard enough.

TASK Sit quietly and close your eyes. Start with a session of Instant
Relaxation described on page xx. Make sure you don't go to sleep! Now,
in your mind's eye, try to construct a perfect sunny day. Choose a location
that you know very well indeed (your garden would be an obvious choice).
Imagine it bathed in sunlight. Adjust your vision as you wish. Is it early
morning light or that lovely orange evening glow? Mentally walk around
the garden and see the flowers. Notice all the shapes and colours. Walk
barefoot on the grass and feel it tickle your soles. Listen to the hum of
insects. Watch the butterflies. Do you have a water feature? Listen to the
water trickling softly. Feel the heat of the sun on your skin.

You can add any other details you want. Maybe you'd like to hear
some of your favourite music playing softly from inside the house, or
perhaps you'd prefer the laughter of children coming from a neighbouring
garden. If you like, sit down in the dappled sunlight light under a tree
and survey your perfect day at your leisure. Do not let any negative
thoughts intrude. This is your perfect garden and worries or nuisances
are not permitted to enter. You can even imagine a KEEP OUT notice
if you want. Keep the exercise up as long as you like and, if you want, go
to sleep when you've had enough.

HELP

Unless you know that you are good at this sort of exercise, you
should prepare yourself by doing a few sessions of Candle Power on
page xx. Try to commit scenes to memory. Fix details in your mind
so that you can use them later on in your visualizations.

Around The House

AIM This is a memory technique that uses visualization. It is useful for remembering a limited amount of information in the short term.

TASK For this exercise you need to see a familiar place, such as your own house, in your mind's eye. Let's say that you need to remember a list of things to do. First you must divide your list into sections, such as things to do at home, at work and social arrangements, and so on. Assign one room of the house to each section. Now, mentally, go into each room and leave yourself a note about each task in a separate place. If you can make the place appropriate to the task, so much the better. For example, if you need to buy your wife an anniversary present, mentally leave a note in your place at the dining table. If you need to complete a report for your boss, leave a note lying on the desk in your study. When you want to recall the information, just visit the appropriate room and pick up the notes.

Cerebrum
The cerebrum is the largest part of the brain and makes up 85% of the brain's weight.

HELP
When you have used the technique you must remember to go around and empty all the locations you no longer need so that they can be used again. You can, of course, always add more locations as the need arises.

RHYTHM AND RHYME

Rhyming is a very powerful memory aid. We can use rhythm and rhyme to cover both metre (as used in poetry) and music. You can use both of these to remember a wide variety of things. Beware! This is a very, very strong glue. Anything you remember this way will stay with you for life.

When no one's listening, try singing the nursery rhyme 'Jack and Jill Went Up the Hill'. Go on! Just for me. One thing I'll guarantee, you haven't forgotten the words or the tune. That's because rhythm and rhyme are very, very, very strong memory glue. If you want to remember something forever, set it to music with a good, strong rhythm. In olden times, the bards would not just tell old stories, they would sing them. That's how they remembered all those interminable tales of heroes, gods and beautiful maidens. If I ask you to tell me a well-known story like, say, Peter Pan, you'll probably be able to give me a précis; but the whole thing, word for word? I doubt it. But you can learn huge chunks of Shakespeare by heart because that's poetry and the rhythm helps you, even though much of the language is unfamiliar.

Instructions

- There is no magic trick to learning things that come with rhythm and rhyme built in. The fact is that our minds naturally store anything that comes in this form. That's why kids can learn endless pop songs and be word perfect in all of them.
- All you have to do is split the thing into chunks
- Just keep going over it until the rhythm and rhyme embed themselves in your memory.

Gray and white
Your brain is 60% white matter and 40% gray matter.

GIVE ME A BREAK!

It is important to take breaks during a memorization task. The mind works in mysterious ways, and one of them is that it keeps on working even when you think it has stopped. If you start a task today, and then stop and get a night's sleep, you'll find that during the night your mind has been mulling over the memory and by the next day your performance will have improved. If you don't take breaks, you'll get tired and stale and your task will be longer and more arduous.

Presidents of the USA

Just for fun let's learn the Presidents of the USA. The first four are easy because they have a natural rhythm. Try saying without Washington, Adams, Jefferson, Madison without introducing a metre – it's almost impossible! The rest will provide more of a challenge:

> Washington, Adams, Jefferson, Madison,
> Monroe and Adams, Jackson, Van Buren,
> Harrison, Tyler, Knox Polk and Taylor,
> Fillmore and Pierce, Buchanan and Lincoln,
> Johnson and Grant, Hayes and Garfield,
> Arthur and Cleveland, Harrison, Cleveland,
> McKinley, Roosevelt, Taft and Wilson,
> Harding and Coolidge, Hoover and Roosevelt,
> Truman and Eisenhower, Kennedy, Johnson,
> Nixon and Ford, Carter and Reagan.
> George Bush, Bill Clinton, George W. Bush
> And Barack Obama.

OK, now trying learning it a couple of lines at a time. Use a really sing-song voice just the way you were taught not to read poetry at school. In half an hour you should have the whole thing. Come back to the task a couple of times over the next few days and again in a couple of weeks' time. You'll find you can do the whole list without a slip.

KINAESTHETICS

The art of kinaesthetics (how weight, movement and touch are perceived by the body) can play an important role in memory. For instance, you learn to play a musical instrument by using your sense of touch. Your fingers remember the correct positions and pressures. Also, you can reinforce other memories by adding some sort of motion to them – some people beat out time while memorizing. You might not want everyone to see you do this (they might just get the wrong idea about your sanity), but it does work.

The gentle touch

Do you remember showing some new possession (a camera, for example) to a friend for the first time? He says, 'Oh, let's have a look!' and takes it from you, apparently to look closer. But as well as looking, he is also feeling. For some reason, we are a bit coy about our habit of learning through touch. We actually would like to touch all sorts of things (especially other people) just to get to know them better, to quite literally get a feel for them. The sense of touch is delicate but also very powerful.

Touch does not just inform us of things that are going on right now, but it also involves a specialized kind of memory. A blind friend once showed me how he could run his fingers over the cards in a pack and identify many of them just by the way they felt: odd irregularities, creases and bent corners, which would be just about invisible to a sighted person, were picked out unerringly by his heightened sense of touch.

Although our sense of touch is innate, like all other senses it can be improved by practice. You need to spend some time quite deliberately feeling objects and trying to identify them just from touch. Some work depends entirely on a well-developed touch memory. For example, a bomb disposal officer is trained to do this sort of work largely by the memory of how things feel. It is not always possible to open up a bomb and take a good look inside, so he needs to be able to feel his way around. A touch in the wrong place could put a very sudden end to his career.

SMELL

Smell is the strongest memory key of all. This is strange when you consider that, compared to other animals, our sense of smell is quite frail. Nevertheless, we have all had the experience of a sudden aroma taking us back to some place we loved or hated years before. Chalk dust can evoke school classrooms, the smell of chlorine conjures up swimming lessons long past, and strawberries have a smell inseparable from hot summer days.

The smell trigger is highly personal. Although most readers will relate to at least some of the smells given off by the items below (because they are very common ones), we all have our own special triggers. I react strongly to the smell of the herb coriander (cilantro). It reminds me of my time teaching in Thailand, when it was served with virtually every meal. It has a powerful smell which, until I was used to it, I found rather offensive. Then I got to like it, and now the smell reminds me of delicious Thai meals I've enjoyed in the past.

It is frustrating that the smell trigger cannot be used to help us store information. It doesn't provoke the right kind of memory. Smell is closely linked to emotion rather than the recall of facts. It might help you to remember places, people, or things that made you happy, sad, angry, lovelorn, or amused; sadly, it cannot remind you of, say, the names of the Presidents of the USA.

Is there any practical use for the smell trigger? It is useful for creating moods (as anyone who owns an oil burner, or who regularly uses incense, will testify). You could use it as an adjunct to other memorization methods by introducing aromas that you find agreeable and which put you in a relaxed mood.

Confidence

Probably when someone gives you an address, phone number or any other important information, you rush at once to write it down. Don't! Learn to have confidence in your memory. The more practice you have at remembering, the more you remember. Have confidence in your ability and you'll soon find that it is justified.

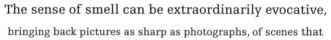

The sense of smell can be extraordinarily evocative,

bringing back pictures as sharp as photographs, of scenes that

had left the **conscious mind**.

Thalassa Cruso, *To Everything There is a Season*

Smelly Souvenirs

AIM Smell is probably the strongest memory trigger there is. The aim of this task is to use that fact to our advantage.

TASK The sense of smell cannot be used to memorize facts, figures, names, faces, etc. It would be wonderful if it could but, for one thing, humans are just not that good at detecting scents and, for another, memories evoked by smell are of a very different type. The sense of smell is excellent for evoking a sense of place. If you are of a certain age the smell of chalk dust will almost certainly drag you back to your school days and it is quite likely that a certain smell will remind you strongly of your childhood home. Such associations are mostly made unconsciously, but there is no reason why that should continue to be so. When you go to new places make yourself consciously aware of how they smell. Take deep breaths and savour the local scent (which, in the case of my fen village, involves large doses of pig manure). You'll find that these smells will act as memory pegs on which you can hang records of your life. It is amazing how a smell will bring back not just a place but the people and events associated with it.

HELP

The sense of smell, like all other senses, can be refined by practice. Just as a wine connoisseur can detect innumerable odours in a fine wine you will, with practice, be able to evoke memories simply be enlisting your sense of smell.

STORYTELLING

I know people who swear by narratives. The method involves making up simple stories that connect a string of objects or facts to be remembered. For example, if you want to remember the telephone number 5231870, you could use a bit of imagination and turn it into, 'At five to three I ate seven cookies.' The trouble is that most information you'll want to memorize will need quite a leap of imagination to turn it into a narrative.

I want to tell you a story

One way of remembering things is to combine them into a silly story. Note the word 'silly'. The sillier the story, the more likely you are to remember it. For example, picture the words in **bold** below as an image in your mind of what they describe (i.e. a golf tee for tea) and you could come up with something like this.

I was walking on stilts
(that looked like **hockey sticks**)

when I **lacrossed** the road and
tripped over a heap of **tennis balls**.

My intentions were **foiled** because
I crashed into a **fence**,

which made an enormous **racket**.

After that I needed some **tea**,

so I went to my **club** to wait (**weight**).

No one offered me a lift so I **ran** home,

which left me feeling full of **bounce**.

Stupid? Undoubtedly. But memorable. Try it out for yourself using a conversation you may have with a friend or family member.

Come up with your own story and I bet that within a few minutes you'll be able to remember the whole list without omitting a single item. This is because your brain has been able to visualise the story and, by doing so, remembers it better.

The only problem with this method is that it does confine you to remembering all the items in the same order. If someone asked you, 'Does the tennis racket come before or after the golf clubs?', you'd probably have to run through the whole story to make sure.

Speed
Information in the brain can be processed as slowly as 0.5 meters/sec or as fast as 120 meters/sec (about 268 miles/hr) depending on what the function is.

KEEP IT WACKY
You don't remember sensible things because they're just too boring. You do remember wacky things. Use wild associations, crazy rhymes, and weird visual images. My father taught me the alphabet by getting me to sing it to the tune of the Ode to Joy from Beethoven's Ninth Symphony. You think that's a crazy thing to teach a little kid? I loved it! Try singing it in the shower and you'll see what I mean.

REPETITION

Repetition is probably the simplest and oldest memory device, but that doesn't mean you should fail to take advantage of it. Simply repeating something over and over to yourself will help to create a memory, though probably not a long-lasting one.

The school kid's trick of learning spellings or multiplication tables last thing at night and then sleeping with the book under their pillow is effective if all you want to do is pass a test the next day, but the memory will soon fade. Sometimes, however, you need to learn something just for a short time and not be burdened with it forever. In that case repetition is an ideal technique. If you want the memory to be stronger, then combine it with one of the other techniques (such as rhyming or association).

Talking telephone numbers

Repetition is great for, say, a telephone number that you need just once. Repeat after me: 0795634. Say it again, and again, and again. If you work at it for a couple of minutes, you'll find that the memory sticks – but not for long. It's doubtful whether, without using some other method, you would be able to remember those numbers this time tomorrow. But that's OK because there are some things we just don't want to remember for very long. So, if you look up a phone number and want to remember it just long enough to get to the phone and punch the buttons, repetition is a good technique. If, however, you've just met someone you think might become the love of your life and have been given his or her phone number, this is not a safe way to commit it to memory.

When my kids were really young, they would prepare for spelling tests by repeating the spellings until they got them all right. In those days, I knew less about memory than I do now, so, because I'd been taught to learn my spellings parrot fashion as well, I went along with it. The result? They both got excellent marks in their spelling tests, BUT by the next week they had forgotten everything they'd supposedly learnt.

Repetition forms part of all the other techniques you will learn and, used in combination with those techniques, it is very powerful; on its own it is only a temporary fix.

There is another important use for repetition, however, and that is in getting other people to remember something. I used to study Spanish at a local community college. People came from surrounding villages; one of which was called Over. Every time anyone mentioned that they came from Over, the teacher would say 'sobre' (the Spanish for 'over'). He said it every lesson and, by the end of the year, if there was one word of Spanish that everyone remembered permanently it was 'sobre'. The limitation of this technique is that you can only get people to remember things they want to remember. If you repeat something they don't want to remember, it'll just bounce off like water off a duck's back. For example, I frequently tell my kids to tidy up and turn off TVs, hair straighteners, CD players, lights and so on before they go to school. Several thousand repetitions have so far failed to do the trick.

Neocortex
The neocortex makes up about 76% of the human brain
and is responsible for language and consciousness. The human
neocortex is much larger than it is in animals.

PLAY IT AGAIN, SAM
Memories that you want to keep fresh should be reviewed
regularly. After you have used the techniques in this book for a
while, you'll build up a library of memories and, from time to
time, you need to test yourself again. You can do this in any
scrap of spare time you have, for example while travelling to
work, or even while doing some other task such as mowing the
lawn or cooking dinner. This reviewing procedure needn't be
boring and can actually be quite a good way to relax and forget
the stresses of the day.

Repeating Shakespeare

Here is a little bit of Shakespeare (from *Henry V, Part 2*). Repeat it out loud and then try it with your eyes shut. Keep doing this until you can remember the whole piece. See how long the memory lasts without any other technique to help strengthen it.

O sleep! O gentle sleep!
Nature's soft nurse, how have I frighted thee,
That thou no more wilt weight mine eyelids down
And steep my senses in forgetfulness?
Why rather, sleep, liest thou in smoky cribs,
Upon uneasy pallets stretching thee,
And hushed with buzzing night-flies to thy slumber,
Than in the perfumed chambers of the great,
Under the canopies of costly state,
And lulled with sound of sweetest melody?

Shakespeare
The word 'brain' appears 66 times in the
plays of William Shakespeare.

PHYSICAL REMINDERS

Aphysical reminder is something such as tying a knot in the corner of your handkerchief to help you remember. All little kids have done this at some time but, just because it's used by little kids doesn't mean that it won't work for you. It will. This method, however, works only briefly (which is all it was meant to do). It will remind you to pick up the kids from school, or take the car to the garage to be fixed, or pick up your dry-cleaning. Once it has accomplished the task, you get rid of it.

There's always something there to remind me]

Physical reminders like this are a quick and easy way to get you to remember something simple that might otherwise slip your mind. Some people use methods such as a rubber band wound around one finger (rather uncomfortable and too obvious) or a sticking plaster covering a non-existent cut.

Physical reminders can be extended from your person to your surroundings. Leaving some familiar object out of its normal place can act as a memory trigger. For most of us, this technique can work at a simple level (car keys left on the coffee table, instead of on the key rack, can tell you to take the car for servicing), but if you leave too many reminders around they might become confusing.

Some families get so used to communicating in this way, that they leave quite complicated 'notes' for each other that no one else could ever understand. For example, someone might leave a stone misplaced near the front door to tell other family members that a spare set of house keys has been hidden in the potting shed. Cunning, eh?

ATTACK ON ALL FRONTS AT ONCE
Don't use just one technique to remember something – try to use several. Looking, listening and doing methods should all be combined for the best result.

EIDETIC MEMORY

What used to be called photographic memory is now known by the term 'eidetic memory'. Some people can look briefly at an object, design or document and then reproduce it in minute detail, just as though their mind had taken a photograph of it. As you would imagine, there is huge controversy surrounding this whole topic. Some psychologists are strong believers in eidetic memory, whilst others have doubts or even deny that there is any such phenomenon.

It seems beyond question that certain individuals do have a greater-than-average ability to remember things they have seen. One of my aunts, who was trained as a dressmaker, had the useful ability to copy any dress after looking at it for only a very short time. She built up a thriving business turning out imitations of dresses she had seen pictured at society weddings, or worn by film stars. A flick through the pages of the gossip magazines or, better still, a few minutes spent in the presence of the actual dress, and she could make you a perfect copy.

The point is, could you learn to do this, or do you have to be born with the ability? Let's see! The drawings on these pages start out as quite simple, but get increasingly complex. Look at each drawing (for as long as you need). Then put the book aside and try to reproduce the drawing in as much detail as possible.

Train your eidetic memory

There are numerous free computer games, available on the Internet to help train your eidetic memory. Simply search under the words 'eidetic memory training' and you will find a wide choice of programs on offer.

TECHNIQUES FOR BETTER RECALL

Whatever techniques you favour, there are a number of things you can do to make memorization more effective. You should always do all of these things if you want to get the very best results.

Divide and conquer

Never try to remember whole chunks of information in one go. Break any large task into a series of smaller ones. If there are natural breaks, so much the better.

Rest and repeat

Don't try to master something in one session. The mind is a funny thing and it goes on working even when we have apparently taken a rest. This process is very important and must be given a chance to work. Work on a memory task for no more than twenty minutes and then put it to one side. Try again the next day, and the next. You can have several tasks ongoing at the same time if you wish. You will find that by resting and revising, you will form very strong memories.

Attack from all sides

Don't always use just one method. I'll show you how to combine several methods for a much better result. If you enjoy listening most, make the Rhyme & Rhythm technique your No. 1 wherever appropriate, but be sure to use other methods in addition. Tap out the rhythm with a pencil. Remember to look, look, look! Visualize what you are trying to remember. Shut your eyes and see the information in your mind's eye. Say the words out loud so that you hear yourself and learn by listening. Repeat, repeat, repeat. Do everything over and over again until you get it perfect. Repetition is not a strong method used on its own but it is highly effective if combined with others.

Review

Review your efforts regularly. You needn't waste valuable time doing this – you can make use of odd moments such as when travelling to work or standing in the shower. These review sessions can be quite pleasurable and they will keep your memories up to date. Even the strongest memory will fade or – even worse – become unreliable if it is not refreshed from time to time.

Take your time

Do not rush memorization. Accuracy is much more important than speed. If you concentrate on accurate memorization, you will build up speed as you get more experienced – you will also be able to remember larger chunks of information at one sitting, when you have practised enough.

Work, don't worry

Getting worried about remembering things is the worst thing you can do. If you work steadily, you will build confidence in your ability to remember and you won't need to worry. If you are revising for an exam, start early. It is much easier to learn material reliably if you can work at it over a period of weeks and months rather than trying to cram it all in at the last minute.

Cerebral cortex

The cerebral cortex – the brain's 'grey matter' – grows thicker as you learn to use it.

MEMORY TIP

Find a bit of time that is underused (such as waiting in heavy traffic) and make that your regular memory review spot.
It will while away a boring part of your day and add something useful to your life.

BUZAN'S TOP 99
GENIUSES AND THEIR IQS

Tony Buzan is a prominent psychology author as well as a leading name in promoting the usage of innovative Mind-mapping and mnemonic techniques, just some of the tricks we have used in this book.

Buzan has written many successful books related to the brain and the notion of 'Genius Quotient' or 'GQ', as well as successful books on memory, age-proofing the brain and speed-reading. From his book, *Buzan's Book of Genius* (1994), Buzan used a series of 12 factors (including originality, academic achievement, life span and dominance in field) to estimate the IQs of many famous historical and living people – many, if not all, of whom we now apply the term 'genius' without even thinking about it and for who some are synonymous with the word.

1. Leonardo Da Vinci 230	20. Marie Curie 180
2. Johann Goethe 210	21. Stephen Hawking 180
3. William Shakespeare 210	22. Plato 180
4. Albert Einstein 205	23. Leon Battista Alberti 180
5. Isaac Newton 195	24. Alexander Graham Bell 180
6. Thomas Edison 195	25. Pitt the Elder 180
7. Thomas Jefferson 195	26. Napoleon Bonaparte 180
8. Aristotle 190	27. Alexander the Great 180
9. Archimedes 190	28. Genghis Khan 180
10. Filippo Brunelleschi 190	29. Ivan Pavlov 180
11. Nicolaus Copernicus 185	30. Phidias 180
12. John Stuart Mill 185	31. Salvador Dali 180
13. Benjamin Franklin 185	32. Igor Stravinsky 180
14. T.S. Eliot 185	33. Queen Elizabeth I 180
15. Gottfried Wilhelm Leibnitz 182	34. Andrew Carnegie 180
16. Euclid 182	35. Mimar Sinan 180
17. Jorge Luis Borges 180	36. Marcel Duchamp 180
18. Galileo Galilei 180	37. Arthur Conan Doyle 182
19. Michael Faraday 180	38. Marion Tinsley 182

39. Rene Descartes 175
40. Michelangelo 175
41. Baruch Spinoza 175
42. Dante 175
43. Homer 175
44. Pablo Picasso 175
45. 1st Ch'in Emperor 175
46. Averroes 175
47. Suli 175
48. Desiderius Erasmus, D. 175
49. Werner Heisenberg 175
50. Bill Gates 173
51. Charles Darwin 173
52. Francis Crick 173
53. Sophocles 173
54. John Milton 173
55. George Stephenson 173
56. Aeschylus 173
57. Euripides 173
58. Lao-Tzu 173
59. Julius Caesar 170
60. Confucius 170
61. Abraham Lincoln 170
62. Raphael 170
63. Guglielmo Marconi 165
64. Frank Lloyd Wright 165
65. Ludwig Van Beethoven 165
66. Machiavelli 165
67. Thomas Aquinas 165
68. Johann Sebastian Bach 165
69. Joseph Lister 165

70. Christopher Wren 165
71. Isambard Kingdom Brunel 165
72. Sun Tzu 165
73. Sappho 165
74. Socrates 160
75. Wolfgang Amadeus Mozart 160
76. Carl Jung 160
77. Suleiman 160
78. Mohandas Gandhi 160
79. Maria Montessori 157
80. Vyasa 156
81. Hannibal Barca 155
82. Field Marshal Earl Alexander 150
83. Giuseppe Francesco Verdi 150
84. Charles Dickens 150
85. Paul Cezanne 149
86. Graham 148
87. Muhammad Ali 147
88. Ferdinand Magellan 145
89. Arthur Wellesley 145
90. Horatio Nelson 145
91. Titan 145
92. Rembrandt 145
93. Jan Zizka 145
94. Johannes Gutenberg 140
95. George Washington 140
96. Christopher Columbus 140
97. Charlie Chaplin 140
98. Morihei Ueshiba 131
99. Walt Disney 123

QUIZ ANSWERS

p19 **Boudicca's Birthday:** There were 129 years between the birth of Cleopatra and the death of Boudicca but as their combined ages came to only 100 year, there must have been 29 years between their lives. Therefore Boudicca must have been born 29 years after the death of Cleopatra in 30BC. This makes the date of her birth 1BC.

p19 **Dear Departed:** Two widows each had a son, and each widow married the son of the other and had a daughter by the marriage.

p20 **What's in a name:** they are all anagrams of girls' names.

p20 **Four Square:** Y. Bottom left x bottom right x top right divided by top left = number of letter in alphabetical order.

p21 **Cross Quiz:** Ben's age is 10 16/21 years, John's is 29 15/21, and Kate's is 24 20/21.

p21 **Day Disorder:** Thursday

p22 **Fifteen Squared:**
2 9 4
7 5 3
6 1 8

p23 **Code Breaker 1:**

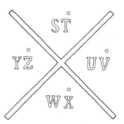

p24 **Code Breaker 2:** We wish you a Merry Christmas. The grid contains all the letters of the alphabet (I and J double up). Co-ordinates are provided by the letters A-E running down the side of the grid and numerals 1-5 along the top.

p24 **Code Breaker 3:** Give peace a chance

p25 **Parts Problem:** C (12), E (14)

p26 **Misfit:** DANDELION is the only one not used as a girl's name

p26 **Flag Figure:** 120

p27 **Letter Pairs: HR:** The others are all equally far apart from each other in the alphabet.

p27 **Nines Answer:** The letters make the word ESPERANTO (the artificial international language).

p28 **Transplantation:**

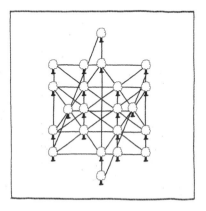

p28 **Delinquent Driver:** There were five people in the men's car, the driver being a woman.

p30 **Prized Possession:** The question leads you to consider decisions that a living person would make. It leads you away from the idea that the subject of the puzzle is dead. Of course, the answer is a coffin.

p31-33 Pub Quiz Answers

QUIZ 1

1.	42	**2.**	12	**3.**	Milliner
4.	Full house	**5.**	Sagittarius	**6.**	The Wealthy
7.	Coca-Cola	**8.**	Richard Nixon	**9.**	1881
10.	Tehran	**11.**	Mali	**12.**	Pele
13.	155	**14.**	Pancreas	**15.**	MACH 1
16.	Long Sightedness	**17.**	Absolute Zero	**18.**	Portuguese
19.	Death	**20.**	1867	**21.**	5%
22.	Crescendo	**23.**	July 14th	**24.**	Atlantic
25.	Greece	**26.**	3	**27.**	Teeth
28.	XIV				

QUIZ 2

A. Four (11, 13, 17 and 19)
B. Obtuse   **C.** 13 (Sum of previous 2 numbers)
D. International Date Line   **E.** 1000
F. 6009   **G.** Trees   **H.** 9
I. Self Contained Underwater Breathing Apparatus   **J.** T for ten
K. Corona   **L.** Denominator   **M.** MCMXCI
N. Makes clocks   **O.** 3   **P.** 7 inches
Q. Salt   **R.** Pen   **S.** 13
T. Hertz   **U.** XCI   **V.** Terrible lizard
W. Peel   **X.** O   **Y.** 23
Z. Binary Digit

Grid 1

2	1			9	4	8		2	9
7	9	4		2	1	5		1	8	2
		2	8	1		9	3		4	1
	2	1	6				2	5	7
6	1		9	8		5	1	3
8	7	3		9	8	3		9	2	1
	5	1		4	2	1			9	8

Grid 2

9	7			2	9			2	1
8	5	9		2	1	3	5		1	3
	1	8		9	3		9	8	3	7
		2	8	4		1	7	2
5	8	4	6		3	9		6	5
3	6		9	2	1	4		9	8	6
2	9		9	7				6	2

Grid 3

7	1			6	9			9	4
9	3	8		2	4	1		6	7	1
	2	4	1	7		2	7	9	8
	1	3			3	1
	8	9	6	4		1	9	8	3
1	7	5		1	4	2		7	2	9
3	5			9	7			1	7

Grid 4

3	1		2	9			9	3	7
8	1	5		1	7		9	8	1	3
9	7			6	1	7	2
	9	1		1	4	2		3	2
		4	9	2	8			3	1
1	3	2	8		5	9		9	8	3
7	9	8			3	7		6	1

Grid 5

9	7		7	1			6	1
6	1		9	2	7		1	2
	2	1		6	9	7	8		4	2
2	5	8	3	4		3	2	1	6	5
1	3		2	3	1	5		6	9
		9	8		4	8	9		7	9
		3	1			1	3		8	5

Grid 6

9	3			6	3		9	7
3	1	2		5	1	2		8	2
		1	3	8	2		7	6	1	2
2	3		8	9	7	5	3		4	9
1	6	9	2		5	3	1	4
	2	6		2	4	1		9	3	8
	1	8		1	3			1	6

Grid 7

9	4			8	9	6			9	8
8	1		4	7	1	3	2		7	9
	7	2	6	9		1	3	9	4
		8	9			1	4
	3	1	8	2		9	4	8	6
8	4		7	3	9	8	6		8	5
3	1			1	2	3			7	9

p101   Lateral Thinking Answers:

The Absent Aunt The sisters were identical twins.

Death of the Dealer He couldn't arrest any of the men – but the dealer was a woman. He arrested her.

Last Supper Mickey was a pet mouse who had escaped and been caught in a mousetrap.

Odd Animals None of them is actually what it says is it. The koala is not a bear, the Bombay duck is not a duck and so on.

Successful Players They were a band employed to play background music.

Sea Story The vessel was Apollo 1, which landed in the Sea of Tranquility on the Moon.

Political Problems They were still in the tin.

p.109   Five Minute Challenge

1.   Table / able.
2.   Wall / all.
3.   Mutter / utter.
4.   Flung / lung.
5.   Lamp / amp.
6.   Clover / lover.
7.   Orange / range.
8.   Frank / rank.
9.   Bark / ark.
10. Taunt / aunt.
11. Pink / ink.
12. Silk / ilk.

 BRAIN FACT

Albert Einstein

Einstein's brain was similar in size to other humans except in
the region that is responsible for math and spatial perception.
In that region, his brain was 35% wider than average.

Created in 2007, Portico publishes a range
of books that are fresh, funny and forthright.

portico

An imprint of Anova Books

WROTTEN ENGLISH

A Celebration of Literary Misprints, Mistakes and Mishaps

Peter Haining

'An absolute gem of a book'

booksmonthly.co.uk

Following on from the hilarious collection of typos, gaffes and howlers in Portico's *A Steroid Hit the Earth*, comes *Wrotten English* – a fabulously funny collection of literary blunders from classic, and not-so classic, works of literature. This book is an anthology of side-splitting authors' errors, publishers' boobs, printers' devils, terrible titles, comical clangers and all manner of literary lunacy dating back since the invention of the printing press.

£9.99 • Hardback • 9781907554100

WHATEVER HAPPENED TO TANGANYIKA?

The Place Names that History Left Behind

Harry Campbell

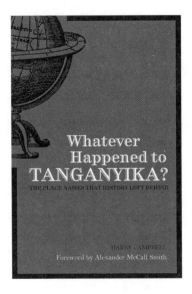

'Marvellous and intriguing, Campbell has
created a whole new discipline – one which
we may perhaps call nostalgic geography.'

Alexander McCall Smith

In this fascinating trawl through the atlas of yesteryear, Harry Campbell
explains how and why the names of countries, cities and counties have
changed over time, and tells the extraordinary tales behind places from
Rangoon to Rutland and Affpiddle to Zaire. *Whatever Happened to
Tanganyika?* is a treasure trove of stories to delight armchair travellers
and history fans alike.

£9.99 • Hardback • 9781906032050

The Hidden Mathematics of Sport

Rob Eastaway & John Haigh

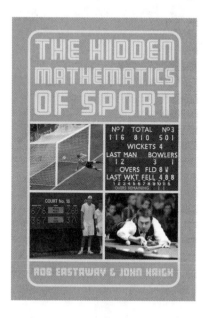

*'A fascinating mixture of analysis, trivia and sporting history,
with plenty to appeal to any sports fan.'*
Ed Smith, *The Times*

The Hidden Mathematics of Sport takes a novel and intriguing look at sport, by exploring the mathematics behind the action. Discover the best tactics for taking a penalty, the pros and cons of being a consistent golfer, the surprising link between boxing and figure skating, the unusual location of England's earliest 'football' game (in a parish church), and the formula for always winning a game of tennis. Whatever your sporting interests, you will find plenty to absorb and amuse you in this entertaining and unique book – and maybe you will even find some new strategies for beating the odds.

£9.99 • Hardback • 9781907554223

365 Reasons To Be Cheerful

Magical Moments to Cheer Up Miserable Sods ... One Day at a Time

Richard Happer

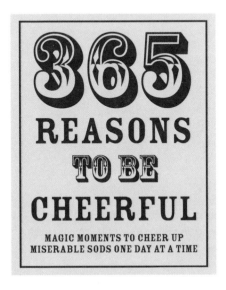

It's a well-observed fact that human beings can be a grumpy old bunch, always choosing to see that infamous metaphorical glass as constantly half empty rather than half full. Where's the fun in that? *365 Reasons To Be Cheerful* is, well, it's exactly that. It's a whole year's worth of funny and unique events that happened on each and every day – a wild, weird and wonderful journey through the year highlighting the moments that changed the world for the better as well as the delightfully quirky stories that will simply make you smile. *365 Reasons To Be Cheerful* is designed specifically to look on the bright side of life every day of the year – the perfect pint-sized pick-me-up in these sobering, sombre times.

£7.99 • Hardback • 9781906032968

'Any man who reads too much and uses his own brain too little falls into lazy habits of thinking.'
Albert Einstein